THE TRACE OF THE FACE IN THE POLITICS OF JESUS

The Trace of the Face in the Politics of Jesus

*Experimental Comparisons Between the Work of
John Howard Yoder and Emmanuel Levinas*

JOHN PATRICK KOYLES

◆PICKWICK *Publications* • Eugene, Oregon

THE TRACE OF THE FACE IN THE POLITICS OF JESUS
Experimental Comparisons Between the Work of John Howard Yoder and Emmanuel Levinas

Copyright © 2013 John Patrick Koyles. All rights reserved. Except for brief quotations in critical publications or reviews, no part of this book may be reproduced in any manner without prior written permission from the publisher. Write: Permissions, Wipf and Stock Publishers, 199 W. 8th Ave., Suite 3, Eugene, OR 97401.

Pickwick Publications
An Imprint of Wipf and Stock Publishers
199 W. 8th Ave., Suite 3
Eugene, OR 97401

www.wipfandstock.com

ISBN 13: 978-1-61097-622-0

Cataloging-in-Publication data:

Koyles, John Patrick.

    The trace of the face in the politics of Jesus / John Patrick Koyles.

    x + 150 p.; 23 cm—Includes bibliographical references and index.

    ISBN 13: 978-1-61097-622-0

    1. Yoder, John Howard. 2. Lévinas, Emmanuel. I. Title.

BX8143.Y59 K69 2013

Manufactured in the USA.

I would like to dedicate this project to Sheri, my beautiful wife, who helped me to finish this project by making extraordinary sacrifices so that I could find the time to write and research as well as encouraging me to finish when I no longer believed I could.

Contents

Acknowledgment | ix

Introduction | 1

1. Following Jesus: Examining John Howard Yoder's Methodological Approach and Conception of Revolutionary Subordination | 9
2. A Sectarian Thinker?: Critical Reflections and Questions Concerning John Howard Yoder's Thought | 31
3. Yoder's Rejoinders: Evaluating the Responses of Yoder's Supporters and Their Employment of the Western Philosophical Tradition | 56
4. The Kenotic Bridge: An Experimental Response Through a Levinasian Rereading of Yoder's Methodology and Revolutionary Subordination | 86

Conclusion | 117

Bibliography | 139

Index | 149

Acknowledgments

I WOULD LIKE TO acknowledge all of my professors and colleagues from the department of Religion at Florida State for all of their kindness and support. I want to especially recognize Drs. Martin Kavka, John Kelsay, Aline Kalbian, and Dan Maier-Katkin for taking the extra time to share their insights as well as their corrective suggestions in helping me see this project to its completion.

Introduction

THE SUBTITLE OF MARK Nation's account of John Howard Yoder's life and thought, *Mennonite Patience, Evangelical Witness, Catholic Convictions*, aptly portrays the impact of Yoder's work. One of Nation's sources of inspiration was William Klassen's tribute to Yoder following his unexpected death.[1] Klassen noted that throughout the numerous memorials offered in the wake of Yoder's death none mentioned the important contribution Yoder made to ecumenical work. Klassen felt that Yoder's efforts to open up Mennonites to the larger Christian tradition had been overlooked. John Howard Yoder had spent a good portion of his life working to open lines of communication between Mennonites and mainstream forms of Christianity. However, Yoder's fame has largely been associated with his work on Christian pacifism and Just War thought. Interestingly, he did contribute to other discourses. For instance, Yoder was interested in exploring with other Christians the contours of a proper model for engaging the world outside of its tradition. Yoder sought to formulate healthy ways of bridging the distance between Christianity and the larger world. Through all of his work Yoder sought to foster an ecumenical dialogue and Klassen believed that even his supportive commentators had fallen into the trap of limiting Yoder's work. Nation's effort to demonstrate the broader nature of Yoder's life and work directly challenges the limited vision of Yoder. This vision describes Yoder as a Mennonite thinker who only provides an articulate account of Christian pacifism. Nation's work, then, is aimed at deepening the portrayal of Yoder beyond his work on Christian pacifism.

---

1. Nation, *John Howard Yoder*, xviii–xix. Klassen's comments are located in his article "John Howard Yoder and the Ecumenical Church," 77–81.

The Trace of the Face in the Politics of Jesus

Nation's book seeks to describe the contours of Yoder's life and thought in order to maintain and extend Yoder's legacy. The limiting view of Yoder's work not only fails to properly articulate the full extent of Yoder's thought, it also restrains that work from future contributions. Nation's work is important because it illuminates the broader aspects of Yoder's thought, providing a clearer account of his insight and demonstrating possibilities for its continued use. One of the gains from Nation's work, aside from the more developed picture of Yoder's life and thought, is the invitation to like-minded scholars to continue to utilize him. Nation's work is not only a memorial to Yoder, it is also an invitation to maintain and extend his legacy.

Even with Nation's excellent work, one is still confronted with the question of how best to go about extending Yoder's thought. The problem is how to develop Yoder's work for future discourse. Again, Nation's book helps by pointing to a possible approach. According to Nation, he would have liked "to have seen Yoder read more philosophy, especially political philosophy."[2] Nation's mention of this point is not to downplay the content of Yoder's work, but to accentuate how it could have been furthered. Nation argues that Yoder's political and philosophical interests, lodged in the interplay between the Christian tradition and its surrounding sociopolitical cultures, are ripe for such a discussion. According to Nation, Yoder's socio-political insights are generated primarily during the 50's and 60's of the twentieth century. This means that they are not readymade for implementation with current political realities. The problem is not contained in the fact that these formulations are generated in the past, it is that some updating and translation is necessary for connecting those insights to current political discourse. The changed context makes it difficult (but not impossible) to extrapolate Yoder's insights from the 50's and 60's onto current political discourse. Nation believes that under the right circumstances these insights can be extracted and used for contemporary discourse. Nation, then, helps to generate a continued interest in Yoder's work by initiating a potential research agenda whereby Yoder's work is to be extended through a conversation with the Western philosophical tradition.

There is, however, a limitation to Nation's work. He is not clear about the nature of this interaction. Nation offers an invitation to extend Yoder's thought, but does not provide guidelines for that proposal. This concern about how to develop Yoder's thought is made more complex by Yoder's conscious effort to avoid extensive use of philosophy (hence Nation's desire

---

2. Nation, *John Howard Yoder*, 198.

Introduction

for more contact). Yoder worried that an alignment between his work and philosophical terminology would risk advocating something other than Jesus as the primary source for Christian theology and ethics. This exchange of Jesus for a philosophical system enabled, in Yoder's mind, human wisdom to supplant the wisdom of God's revelation. Philosophy could substantively transform interpretations of the life and thought of Jesus. Christian salvation would no longer depend on Jesus because one could access this salvation through a clever set of philosophical proofs and arguments. This hesitancy to use philosophy is clearly evident in Yoder's discussion of Jesus' political vision.[3] When Christians come together to discuss their engagement with the larger societal order they overlook the life and message of Jesus as a fundamental source for those talks.[4] According to Yoder, the Christian tradition turned to other sources, like philosophy, to set forth the guidelines for their engagement. Yoder worked hard to try and overthrow this line of reasoning because it sought to locate the primary source for Christian thought and practice beyond the Jesus story. Yoder's work stands as a concerted effort to reprioritize Jesus as the central norm for Christian thinking and living.

This hesitancy, however, should not be viewed as an absolute refusal to engage the Western philosophical tradition. Although one is hard pressed to locate Yoder's encounters with philosophy, it is not impossible. In fact, in his *The Christian Witness to the State* Yoder employs the concept of "middle axioms."[5] These axioms are efforts at developing a line of communication between the Christian tradition and the wider world. Yoder's point is that at certain times one can locate an overlap of interest between these alternative positions. His argument for middle axioms, then, is a way for Christians to speak to the wider world without compromising their identity. In *Body Politics*, Yoder argues that certain practices of the Christian tradition overlap with goals and practices of the wider world.[6] According to Yoder, when Christians perform practices like communion or baptism they are not only engaging in the worship of their deity, but are also performing sociopolitical functions. In other words, the Christian community is not unlike other

---

3. I think that one could effectively argue that the Yoderian corpus is one large effort to articulate Jesus' political vision, but the most concentrated work toward this end is *The Politics of Jesus*.

4. Ibid., 4–14. Yoder provides no less than six reasons for why Christians eschew Jesus as a model of political interaction.

5. Yoder, *Christian Witness to the State*, 32–33, 35–44.

6. Yoder, *Body Politics*.

types of community. Christian practices contain social aspects that can be translated into non-Christian terms. Sociology, then, becomes a translating medium for communication between Christians and that wider world. What the Christian tradition does can be communicated across its boundaries to the outside world in terms that make sense without jeopardizing the Christian nature of that practice.

The combination of Nation's invitation and Yoder's cautious, but present interaction with non-Christian sources creates a fertile ground for placing Yoder into conversation with thinkers from other traditions. This combination does not provide definitive guidelines for that conversation, but it doesn't rule it out either. This project, then, is an experimental and exploratory effort to pursue such a conversation. Like Nation, I agree that Yoder's work can and should remain as an integral component of future Christian discourse. I also concur that Yoder's lack of engagement with philosophy possess a potency for demonstrating its continuing relevance. I believe that linking Yoder with aspects and thinkers of the Western philosophical tradition is important for at least two reasons. First, as Nation has argued, the extension of Yoder's work through a philosophical grid will help to maintain its relevancy. Yoder's insights, which appear to be limited to a bygone era, can contribute to current discourse, but will need to be teased out. Placing Yoder into conversation with philosophy can help to facilitate that work. Also, this effort should be viewed as part and parcel of the larger Christian endeavor to engage its surrounding sociopolitical contexts. The desire, then, to link Yoder to the Western philosophical tradition is firmly placed within the larger Christian tradition. The Christian tradition, whether it likes it or not, cannot avoid engaging its social milieu; it will continue to discuss the boundaries of its identity and its responsibilities toward its neighbors. Yoder's work, if it is to remain a factor, must also wrestle with this reality. Second, the insights embedded in Yoder's work do have continuing relevance. The link between Yoder and various elements of philosophy will demonstrate that relevance. Not only will Yoder's thought continue to be important, but it will also reach beyond the limiting vision of his current interpreters. This effort will yield insights that press beyond questions of pacifism and put forth competent responses to his critics. I will show that Yoder's thought contains trajectories that aid the continuing Christian work of dialoguing with its neighbors.

I have chosen the French philosopher Emmanuel Levinas as a conversation partner for Yoder. I believe that rereading Yoder's work through

Introduction

a Levinasian lens will tease out the insights of Yoder's thought while maintaining his authenticity. One of the merits of Levinas' work is his analysis of the role Western thought has played in creating the violent atrocities of Western culture. According to Levinas, this violence is predicated on the proclivity of Western thought to subsume, through philosophical systematization, the other person. The dissolution of the other person has led to a constant forgetting of one's responsibilities to her. The philosophical work of Levinas is, then, best characterized as a proposal for starting from the perspective of the other. Levinas sought to articulate the priority of ethics. Responsibility to the other person takes precedence over the thematizing work of philosophical systems. There are, then, important parallels between Levinas' analysis of Western thought and Yoder's articulation of Jesus' political vision. These parallels, though, are not fully reducible to one another; yet, Levinas' framework of otherness can help to tease out and communicate Yoder's insights. The heart of my argument, then, is that one can discern a "philosophy of otherness" residing in the work of Yoder. Rereading Yoder in terms of otherness is not only productive for translating his insights it is also capable of maintaining the integrity of his commitment to Jesus as the primary resource for Christian thought and practice.

The trajectory of this argument will play out in four phases. First, I locate and describe two aspects of Yoder's work: Yoder's methodology (or lack thereof) and revolutionary subordination. This will set out the parameters of the conversation. It also illuminates the need for extending his thought. These two elements are important because they demonstrate Yoder's hesitancy to engage philosophical sources and contain the latent inherent potential for such engagement. Their controversial nature and the lack of supplemental supportive argumentation provide fuel for reading Yoder in limiting terms. This phase indicates the need for rereading Yoder by attending to two places where both his limitations and possibilities coexist.

The second phase further develops the need for linking Yoder to philosophical thought by examining his work through the eyes of his critics. The thinkers covered in this section highlight the limited nature of his work and bolster the claim that he is largely an interesting thinker but retains very little relevance outside of discussions of pacifism and Just War. These thinkers work out of the conception that Yoder's work is largely "sectarian," thereby making it of little value beyond its limited scope. Reading Yoder's work as a sectarian thinker indicates that it is largely a posture of withdrawal or avoidance of the wider world. Many of Yoder's supporters, as well as himself, strenuously worked to overturn this interpretation.[7] They argued that characterizing Yoder in this way is a failure to fully examine him. In their minds, the "sectarian" label becomes an easy way of writing off Yoder without having to take him seriously. The effort to highlight Yoder's critics' use of the "sectarian" label, however, is a two-edged sword. The same criticism of not reading too closely can be turned back onto Yoder's supporters with regard to their reading of his critics' work. It is also an injustice to claim that their work is only motivated by the "sectarian" interpretive scheme. There is a deeper aspect to their criticism of Yoder. Although they may seem to easily write him off, their work indicates a need for demonstrating more clearly why it should be accepted. The reach for the sectarian label may be produced by an inability to fully understand the nature of his work; not because they don't read it, but because it seems difficult to understand. This second section further clarifies the need to reread Yoder.

The third phase turns from demonstrating the need for this project toward viewing current efforts by prominent Yoderian scholars to fill that void. While the first two phases set out the need for linking Yoder to the Western philosophical tradition, this section examines some current attempts to explore an extension of Yoder through conversations with thinkers of that tradition. I have chosen to view the work of Craig Carter, Stanley Hauerwas, and Chris Huebner for this section. Their work on Yoder speaks for itself, but, even more importantly, each thinker has offered important responses to Yoder's critics by linking him with thinkers within the Western philosophical tradition. Their efforts to extend Yoder's legacy in this way serves as a further validation for my own project. I have two purposes, then, for this section of the paper. First, the examination of their work serves to buttress my own. We see that Nation's invitation is already being worked out. Carter, Hauerwas, and Huebner have already taken up this invitation by rereading Yoder in terms outside of his work. My project, then, is a continuation of this impulse. I, like them, perceive the continuing value and insight of Yoder's thought. In a similar manner, I am also extending Yoder by linking him with thinkers and concepts beyond his original scope. The main point of difference between myself and these others is not

---

7. One of the clearest examples of this effort is his book *For the Nations* where he argues not only that Christians ought to engage their wider societies but also provides insight for registering such interactions. Two of the three supporters to be viewed in this paper, Stanley Hauerwas and Craig Carter, put forward an argument against this portrayal of his work (as well as their own).

Introduction

whether to reread Yoder, it is, instead, the answer to the question "with whom." This leads to the second purpose of this section. Along with highlighting the contours of their extension of Yoder, especially their successful responses to his critics, I look at what limitations their work places back onto Yoder's thought. These limits are not lodged in their efforts to redeem Yoder in the face of his critics (in fact, I will largely view their work as offering a persuasive response to his critics); rather they appear to transform Yoder's purposes. In order to provide a compelling response to his critics, they sacrifice integral aspects of Yoder's thought. The problem isn't that they want to respond to his critics, but it is with whom they utilize to draw out that response. The limitations of their effort are embedded in their misconstruing of Yoder's aims and themes; Carter, Hauerwas, and Huebner offer a compelling and persuasive set of responses to Yoder's critics, but only at the expense of important elements of his work.

The final phase of the argument is to make the connection between Yoder and Levinas. To this point, the argument has worked toward demonstrating the legitimacy of this project and illustrating the need for a productive framework for rereading Yoder. This section of the project will make the case for viewing Levinas' thought as fulfilling that need. I will begin by highlighting two aspects of Levinas' work: his critique of Western philosophy (namely, its penchant for ontological reasoning) and his phenomenological description of the encounter with the face of the other. It is my contention that these two components can help to draw out the insights of Yoder's methodological approach and his call for the practice of revolutionary subordination. I will argue that the bridge for connecting Yoder with Levinas is the concept of kenosis. Although this concept is largely identified with the Christian theological tradition, Levinas periodically demonstrates its appearance and value for both his philosophical work and Judaism.[8] Kenosis, in his view, was another way of getting at his elucidation of the encounter with the other person. Levinas' link between kenosis and the face to face encounter drew out the social and political ramifications of that concept. Kenosis is not a grand theological scheme but rather the interruption of the subject's world through the humiliating approach of the other. The bridge, then, is not only strengthened by Levinas' willingness to operate with this term, but also by Yoder's insistence

---

8. See his articles "A Man-God?" in *Entre Nous: Thinking-of-the-Other*, 53–60; "Judaism and Kenosis" and "Judaism and Christianity" in *Levinas: In the Time of the Nations*, 101–18, 145–50.

to read kenosis beyond individualizing notions of inner piety. For Yoder, kenosis was a sociopolitical strategy performed by Jesus. The meditation of the "self-emptying" of God wasn't merely food for thought, but a plan of action. For both, then, the concept is a posture—a way of being-in-the-world. This linkage then allows me to reread Yoder's methodological approach and revolutionary subordination in terms of a philosophy of otherness. Restating these two concepts in terms of "otherness" offers a way of responding to his critics without losing the authenticity of his original aims and themes. One does not have to abandon or apologize for these characteristics of Yoder's thought. They are now recast in a way that enables them to continue to speak—to be valuable for contemporary sociopolitical discourse. The final portion of this section is to provide an answer to his critics while maintaining a commitment to the authenticity of his perspective.

The conclusion will briefly summarize the arguments of this project. It will stitch together the constitutive elements seeking to create a holistic picture. I will also briefly point out three remaining questions. The link between Yoder and Levinas is not without tension. These remaining questions are an indication of my recognition of that tension. The tumultuous history between the Christian and Jewish traditions, the nature and uses of violence, and the feminist critique of "other-centered" ethical approaches arise from this project. The effort to answer these questions pushes beyond the scope of this project. Nevertheless, just because they are outside the parameters of this project it should not undermine their importance. I want to briefly sketch out, in the conclusion, the nature of these questions as well as some initial pathways toward resolving them. These comments, then, are more an invitation for further reflection rather than an attempt to fully resolve them. This project is part and parcel of the larger desire, indicated by the work of people like Mark Nation, Stanley Hauerwas, Craig Carter, and Chris Huebner, to see the continued use and development of Yoder's thought. Although Yoder's unexpected death signaled an end to his illustrious career, it is imperative that his supporters continue to develop his work for future Christian theological and ethical reflection.

chapter one

Following Jesus

Examining John Howard Yoder's Methodological Approach and Conception of Revolutionary Subordination

Introduction

THE CONFUSION AND LACK of interest that have limited the use of John Howard Yoder's thought is better ascertained through a close examination of his work. This chapter looks at two aspects of his thought: his methodological approach and his description of the practice of revolutionary subordination. These two aspects have been chosen for two reasons. First, they are controversial. Their controversial nature is perfect for setting out the reasons for his critics' unwillingness to expand their use of his work. Yoder's advocacy of these elements creates a recalcitrant nature to his work; his critics find these aspects a bit off-putting. Second, these two aspects offer a window into the heart of Yoder's work. His methodology contains a necessary link with his promotion of revolutionary subordination. This linkage is predicated on a deeper conceptual perspective. Examining these two in detail unveils that deeper perspective. Yoder's methodology and his articulation of revolutionary subordination are derivatives of this encompassing perspective and the examination of each enables one to perceive the potential link with Levinas.

Yoder's work is best understood as an attempt to elucidate the concept of Christian discipleship. Yoder's work is largely an effort, then, to articulate the Christian call to follow Jesus. Yoder's methodology and his notion of revolutionary subordination are intricately tied to this larger aim. This chapter contains three trajectories. First, it will describe each of these aspects. Second, it will illuminate the link between these particular ideas and his larger effort to articulate Christian discipleship. Finally, the chapter will locate various points where these elements are at work in his thought. The overarching goal, then, is to gain a competent grasp of Yoder's concepts and to perceive their place in his larger corpus. This will illuminate both the difficulty and potential inherent in his thought.

Yoder's Methodology and Revolutionary Subordination: A Restatement

Yoder's Methodology

Craig Carter suggests that two characteristics make his work difficult to implement.[1] First, it is voluminous. Yoder was prolific. His published works alone are copious. He wrote to a wide range of audiences, both academic and layperson readers. The sheer volume of his work, then, contributes to the difficulty of grasping the whole of his corpus. The second characteristic is his style. According to Carter, "Yoder wrote no major systematic treatise in which the comprehensiveness, logical rigor, and originality of his theology could be readily ascertained."[2] Carter's comment indicates that the difficulty of reading Yoder is that he is too scattered and not general enough to draw out concrete observations. Reading Yoder is difficult because where it fit in the larger scheme of Christian theological and ethical reflection was not readily apparent. What his critics miss, however, is that Yoder had a method to his madness; he purposely wrote in this manner because this style embodied the message he sought to convey. Yoder resisted writing a comprehensive treatise because he saw such work as eliminating conversations. He believed his style better communicated this desire to cultivate dialogue and the eschewal of writing a comprehensive treatise was a derivative of this commitment to writing in dialogical terms.

Stanley Hauerwas confirms this commitment to dialogue, commenting that "his work was always a dialogue…He never wanted to do anything that was self-generating."[3] The closest that John Howard Yoder might have

1. Carter, *Politics of the Cross*, 17–18.
2. Ibid., 18.
3. Hauerwas and Huebner, "History, Theory, and Anabaptism: A Conversation on

come to writing a systematic treatise was his famous book *The Politics of Jesus*. Even here, however, many of the chapters are limited to the discussion regarding the proper place of the Jesus narratives for theological and ethical thinking. Yoder's essay on patience, "'Patience' as Method in Moral Reasoning,"[4] is another portrayal of Yoder's desire to write conversationally. One of the chief themes running through this work is the importance of maintaining a posture that fosters dialogue. This posture is so important that some of the examples he provides indicate that one give space for his interlocutor to speak, even if this means giving her the first and last word. This commitment to a conversational style makes interpreting Yoder's work difficult because each essay is only a limited piece of what is taking place in his mind. This did not mean that Yoder wrote an article that completely rejected or contradicted portions from his earlier work. Nevertheless, making the connections between his various articles remains a difficult enterprise.

Within his conversational strategy Yoder developed two important elements: a straightforward reading of the Bible and a suspicion toward reducing Christian theological and ethical reasoning solely into philosophical categories. Yoder opens up his work *The Politics of Jesus* with this comment. "It (TPOJ) claims not only that Jesus is, according to the biblical witness, a model of radical political action, but that this issue is now generally visible throughout New Testament studies."[5] Yoder argues here that the politics of Jesus can be readily ascertained by reading the "biblical witness;" one doesn't need to address outside sources, one only needs to open to the canonical Gospels. Yoder's reference to "New Testament studies" is a validation of this return. The radical nature of Jesus is detectable through a straightforward reading of the text and New Testament scholars have confirmed this. Even with all of the valuable insights that Yoder produces in *The Politics of Jesus*, one aspect that is often missed is his reassertion of the biblical record as a primary source for Christian theological and ethical reflection. Yoder believed that one could perceive Jesus' political vision by merely reading the texts of the Bible. Alongside of this stated claim is Yoder's implied criticism that people have overlooked this simple fact because they have been blinded by their prior assumptions and presuppositions about these texts. In other words, the straightforward reading of the texts

---

Theology after John Howard Yoder" in *Wisdom of the Cross*, 391.

4. Yoder, "'Patience' as Method in Moral Reasoning: Is an Ethic of Discipleship "Absolute" in *Wisdom of the Cross*, 24–42.

5. Yoder, *Politics of Jesus*, 2.

has been discarded in favor of placing the concepts and categories of a philosophical framework as the proper interpretive grid for reading through these texts. This leads, according to Yoder, to the position that Jesus is either irrelevant (i.e. he is not interested in politics) or impractical (i.e. what he offers is impossible to implement) for engaging in socio-ethical discourse. Yoder's approach counters this thinking by reinstalling the Bible as the primary source for doing theological and ethical work and by rejecting the necessity of filtering that reading through a prearranged philosophical grid.

Yoder's effort to return to the Bible is more complex than it first appears. At first glance, he appears to want to skip over the hermeneutical issues that often plague the interpretation of ancient texts. His descriptions of his reading style, however, indicate that he is well aware of these thorny issues and that the implementation of the finest critical tools is very much a part of his effort.[6] Yoder likens his strategy to a hermeneutical approach known as "Biblical Realism."[7] Yoder describes three vital aspects to this approach: the implementation of all current literary methods for interpretation, an *a priori* acceptance of the authority of the canonical biblical texts, and an emphasis on perspective over against propositional content. These elements clearly illuminate a depth to Yoder's approach.

Yoder's work, contrary to many opinions, was deeply influenced by the scholarly tools of interpretation. Yoder's concerns about those tools lay mostly with the users rather than the tools themselves. Yoder's notion of a "straightforward" style of reading is more directed at the way in which one approaches the biblical record. Yoder retells the story of the numerous quests for the historical Jesus, which continually ended in failure.[8] In fact, many of these quests ended up producing material that countered their claims rather than confirming their initial insights. For Yoder, however, this failure does not necessitate the removal of the tools that were used to conduct these quests. One of the handicaps of these efforts was the initial biases held by the scholars prior to their engagement with the texts. Yoder turns to the work of Albert Schweitzer to illuminate this development. Prior to Schweitzer's work, many scholars (Yoder names Harnack) pictured Jesus as "a sweetly reasonable and enlightened teacher of monotheism, designating God as a loving father."[9] All of this changed, however, when Schweitzer res-

---

6. *Politics of Jesus* is a demonstration of this fact. He buttresses the claims of that text with, then, current New Testament scholarship.

7. Yoder, "The Message of the Bible on its own Terms" in *To Hear the Word*, 125–144.

8. Ibid., 125–27.

9. Ibid., 126.

urrected the eschatological/prophetic nature of Jesus' ministry and teaching. Schweitzer's work discounted the picture of the "sweetly reasonable" Jesus by reinserting the doom and gloom of the eschatological nature of his teaching. Schweitzer's recasting of Jesus as an eschatological prophet exposed, in Yoder's opinion, the assumptions and presuppositions of the earlier questers. They saw Jesus in that way because it derived from what they already believed him to be. Yoder's point, though, is that the problem did not lie with the tools. The idea of a straightforward reading of the texts, then, is not a simple attempt to circumvent the hermeneutical questions and tools, but rather a call to allow the texts to speak for themselves. Yoder's call for a return to the Bible is about placing the voices of those texts on an equal footing with the investigator. His method discourages the subjugation of the texts to the interpreters' prior filtering framework. This means, then, that the interpretive tools are more than welcome, they are required.

The acceptance of the tools and the importance of shelving one's presuppositions points to the second aspect: an acceptance of biblical authority. Yoder argues that it is unnecessary for having to put forth an external argument that lends credibility to the Christian tradition's choice to make the biblical record central to their thinking and practice. He likens the constant attention to proving the authority of the canon to an argument about the necessity of the ground floor of a building.[10] The necessity of the ground floor can be articulated from a variety of angles, but "any one of them looks a little silly when spelled out."[11] Obviously the ground floor is necessary for the building of a building, but it seems ridiculous to have to constantly put forward an argument for its priority and inclusion to that task. This is not to side-step the question of biblical authority (which doesn't seek to discover whether the Bible is authoritative or not, but rather how it is so), it is, though, an attempt to avoid that methodological approach that constantly seeks to reaffirm the priority of these texts.

Yoder does, however, offer an argument for the authority of the Bible. His view on the matter cuts across the two most common answers provided for its authority: the inspiration of the texts or an inspired selection process.[12] In both cases, according to Yoder, the problem is that each fails to recognize the contour of the processes embedded in the generation of the texts themselves. The inspirational view lifts the question up out of history

---

10. Yoder, "The Use of the Bible in Theology" in *To Hear the Word*, 71–84.
11. Ibid., 71.
12. Yoder, "The Authority of the Canon" in *To Hear the Word*, 85–106.

by asserting its authority in terms of a supernatural theory. This viewpoint fails to account for the reality of the later Christian effort to constitute a firmer canon. The supernatural theory doesn't offer an explanation as to how these later Christians were able to discern between those texts which were inspired and those that were not; removing the question from history ends up creating more problems than it solves. The other response, the effort to ground the authority of the canon in the historical selection process, does overcome some of the problems presented by the inspirational view by reinserting the warrants for biblical authority back into history. The problem, however, is that it fails to account for the shifting makeup of the Christian community. In other words, the differences between the earliest communities and the later ones would tarnish the effort to articulate why the texts are authoritative. The failure of this position is lodged in its false belief that the Christian community is unchanging. As Yoder notes, "the Church which confirmed the authority of the texts, in the course of the early centuries, was not the same as the first century church which wrote them, nor as the Roman hierarchy presenting this claim in the seventeenth century."[13] Whereas the inspirational theories tried to escape history, the selection process advocates flattened it into a monolithic constant. In the end, neither viewpoint solves the question – one overlooks the issue completely while the other articulates an unmediated thread of authority through history.

The authority of the Bible is better grounded, according to Yoder, in terms of the thinking process of the earliest Christian communities. The accountability of the claim that the biblical record is primary lies with that first community. "The development of a selection of writings, recognized as authoritative by the churches, *constitutes the final proof,* delivered by the church itself, that the church does not claim final authority but rather subjects herself to the witness of the apostolic age."[14] The New Testament is the effort to articulate in an ever changing world what it means to be faithful to the person they believed to be the messiah. It is this initial decision to subject themselves to these witnesses that makes the Bible authoritative; the texts embody this effort to be faithful – they are the effort to articulate a set of criteria that maps out the boundary lines of the community. The authoritative nature is embedded in the willingness of the community to be subject

---

13. Ibid., 93.

14. Ibid., 94 (italics mine); Yoder draws this statement from the work of Oscar Cullmann's book *Early Church*.

to those criteria. The development of the canon, then, is the later Church's effort to subject itself to that process found in these particular documents. Authority, then, is attached neither to the texts themselves nor to a flattened view of history it is lodged in the initial willingness to be subject to "the witness of the apostolic age."

Yoder's article "The Hermeneutics of Peoplehood: a Protestant Perspective"[15] and his treatise *Body Politics*[16] draw greatly from this conceptualization of biblical authority. The process, which is argued and explicated in more detail in these two texts, is, according to Yoder, the same for any kind of social group. The content and practices are different, but the process of forming a community and the necessary practices to maintain the identity of that community as it moves through history is not solely Christian. The communal process, for Yoder's Biblical Realism, grounds his above claim that the Bible has authority. The key element is that the authority neither rests in some kind of "spiritualized" theory about the inspiration of the Bible nor in the latter Church's selection of those texts. The authority of the Bible is embedded within the communal process of remembering that Jesus is Lord, which leads to the effort to articulate what that looks like in each new contextual setting. The biblical record stands as a guide or criterion for aiding this process.

This move from content to process as the grounds for the authority of the Bible serves as a window into the final aspect of Yoder's Biblical Realism. The effort of this approach is not to turn the biblical record into timeless propositional truths but rather to attempt to lift out the perspective or posture embedded within the texts themselves. For Yoder, the biblical record presents a posture, a way of orienting oneself within the world. This orientation is most important because it guides the quest to be faithful in the ever changing landscape. His reading of these texts, then, is more about adopting a particular point of view rather than trying to locate and articulate clear and distinct sets of rules. *The Politics of Jesus* is an example of this approach. Yoder's articulation of the story of Jesus is an attempt to map out Jesus' orientation to the world. Certainly this orientation carries particular kinds of practices (e.g. pacifism), but these practices are founded on the "axiomatic attitudes and convictions"[17] embedded in the text. Yoder's

---

15. Yoder, "The Hermeneutics of Peoplehood: A Protestant Perspective" in *Priestly Kingdom*, 15–45.

16. Yoder, *Body Politics*.

17. Yoder, "The Use of the Bible in Theology" in *To Hear the Word*, 130.

claim is not that Jesus directly instituted the idea of pacifism. That is, Yoder doesn't picture Jesus sitting his disciples down and directly teaching them to be pacifists. The straightforward reading of the text, however, indicates that something like pacifism must be at work. In other words, the life and message of Jesus point to an orientation to the world that is best characterized in terms of pacifism. Yoder points to Jesus' refusal to take up the Zealot option as an example of this. Jesus' refusal becomes a window into the logic circulating behind his life and thought. The orientation lodged in Jesus' refusal to cooperate with the Zealot movement continues to instruct the Christian tradition to locate alternative forms of engagement. This is the heart of Yoder's approach to the Bible.

One clearly perceives the deeper aspect of his simple call to return to the biblical record. For Yoder, the Bible stands as the primary document for Christian theological and ethical reflection. The centrality of this record, however, is not because it is a book of timeless propositions. Its primacy is contained in the fact that it is the earliest record of Christian efforts to seek what it means to be faithful to Jesus. The Bible is a testament to Christian theological and moral reflection and it details a process that contemporary Christians can imitate. It embodies an orientation toward the world that continues to influence contemporary Christian thought and practice. The quest for faithfulness is, in Yoder's opinion, the timeless mark of the Christian tradition.

Yoder's effort to tie his thinking back to the biblical record is one of the factors that make him so interesting. Another factor is his suspicion of the use of philosophical schemes for restating Christian claims. Yoder believed that the use of a philosophical framework would do more damage than good. The attempt to link Christian claims with a philosophical framework would undermine the nature of the claims as well as the identity of the communities making those claims. The primary danger is how the philosophical framework easily moves from a position of service to one of superiority. The particularity of Jesus is made unnecessary once one is able to completely restate Christian claims in philosophical terms. The content and experience of the Christian faith can be expressed without having to resort to its founder.

Yoder's critical remarks regarding the obsessive concern of Christian theological and ethical discourse with methodology embody his suspicion of philosophical work. He calls this obsession "methodologism."[18]

18. Yoder, "Walk and Word: The Alternatives to Methodologism" in *Theology Without Foundations*, 77–90.

Methodologism is basically "a search for first principles."[19] Yoder's claim is that this effort is more than the task of clarifying one's starting point or terminology. Methodologism is the effort to secure a comprehensive foundation or language for the discourse. Clarification and definition are certainly part of that work, but a secondary move is also present. The secondary feature is the endeavor to locate and explicate a universal or essential nature of the topic. It is this second step that Yoder finds problematic.

Yoder argues that the search for first principles is plagued by an inability to achieve its end. For him, the location of a universal starting point is elusive. Yoder has argued in numerous places[20] that the "exercise of ramification, breaking each question down into subquestions, *will never reach a plateau.*[21] All efforts, then, to reach the Archimedean point are futile. One can always generate another question or concern that will deepen the search. Yoder turns to the topic of lying to demonstrate this futility. Crediting Epictetus, Yoder argues against his claim that philosophy essentially boils down to three questions: that we ought not to lie? Why we ought not to lie? And why that counts as a demonstration?[22] Yoder points out that these questions easily break down into subquestions. In fact, one can raise a multitude of subquestions before one ever moves from the first to the second general question. In other words, one can spend lifetimes trying to figure out what counts as a lie or why it is claimed that one ought not to lie before she ever gets to the question about what counts as a demonstration for the force of the second question. Questioning is never finalized; a new question can always be raised.

The danger, however, goes beyond this inability to reach an end to the questioning. This deeper issue is associated with how the search reshapes the discourse and its participants. The investigation for an absolute starting point often narrows the forms of moral reasoning. Plurality and complexity are viewed as obstacles to be cleared because they invite the problems of skepticism and relativism. The plurality of moral reasoning is viewed as a deterrent because it offers too many different answers to the proposed set of questions. The answer for why one should decide a particular path over

19. Ibid., 77.

20. Ibid.; see also "'But We Do See Jesus': The Particularity of Incarnation and the Universality of Truth" in *Priestly Kingdom*, 46–62; "On Not Being Ashamed Of The Gospel: Particularity, Pluralism, and Validation" in *Faith and Philosophy*, 285–300.

21. Yoder, "Walk and Word: The Alternatives to Methodologism" in *Theology Without Foundations*, 79 (italics mine).

22. Ibid., 77–79.

another appears to reduce to mere assertion and opinion. Methodologism's commitment to locating the essential/universal starting point cannot allow for a plurality of approaches. Plurality and complexity are viewed as hindrances to this project.

This effort to narrow thinking and speaking into a more uniform mode produces serious consequences for Christian communities. This narrowing leads to two further concerns: the primacy of abstract theory over concrete practice and a loss of the community's identity. First, it places methodological reasoning above the "social fabric" of human experience. The Christian community is reduced to an abstract theory; its particularity is downplayed for the greater good of a unifying theme. Turning again to Yoder's examination of lying, he illuminates how discussion about lying fails to account for actual concrete practices of lying and truth-telling. Human experience is considered a distraction to this process because it muddies the work of reason. The task of methodologism is to abstract the essence of lying in order to attain a definition that will stand over against human experience. In order to get at why one ought not to practice lying, one must bracket off the actual practice of lying. This is performed in order to retrieve the essential nature of a lie. The issue with this approach is the way it overlooks the complexity and richness of actual communities. It employs numerous strategies to compartmentalize the dynamic fabric of human existence. People and places are put into service for the concepts; their experience is reduced to a systematic framework where everyone has his/her proper place and function.

The second element derived from the move to abstraction is the evaporation of communal identity. Because the search prioritizes theory over practice the normal distinctive marks of a community's identity are seen as hindrances to the investigation. According to Yoder, the particularity of these communities, especially the rich plurality of their modes of moral reasoning, is funneled into one form. The attempt to rank different strategies of moral reasoning becomes a judgment of the experience of real people. The narrowing of difference results in suspicion and distrust. The plurality of reasoning is viewed as something to be fixed. This forces the community to mold itself to the governing theory; the result is the subsuming of communal identity into the criteria set forth in that theory.

Yoder's final evaluation of methodologism is that it is a form of idolatry. The idolatry is not found in the endeavor to clarify and define what one is trying to say, it is, rather, found in the presumption that one has found the right way to say it. Yoder views discussions about moral reasoning as helpful for clarifying actual moral cases, but when it moves to dominate the discussion by asserting one set of criteria as absolute it moves away from elucidation to idolatry. Idolatry, here, is not the creation of false images for worship but the grasping for power to set forth the conditions by which knowledge and activity are to be adjudicated.[23] It is the presumption of this power and authority to impose its views in an absolute manner. The idolatry is that the conceptual framework stands as the final arbitrator of human experience; this eclipses the dynamic and divergent elements of moral reasoning and human activity. This presumption is viewed by Yoder as a type of violence because it demands that the community curb its identity to participate. Although this form of violence is mostly intellectual, it can be physically forced on the community (it can, at least, provide the impetus for the use of force).

Yoder's reading of Babel illuminates his claim about the violent nature of methodologism.[24] Yoder begins by stating that Stout's *Ethics After Babel*[25] is on the right track when he condemns the violence propagated by an *a priori* attempt at unification. In this manner, Yoder finds common ground with Stout's initial claims. Yoder takes issue with Stout, however, because he fails to see that violence is not eliminated by proposing a process of unification from a different route. According to Yoder, Stout's condemnation is pointed at how the unity is first articulated and then forcibly implemented. Stout's call for the practice of *bricolage* is an attempt to avoid this "a priori" endeavor. *Bricolage* is different from the tower of Babel because the unity is brought about through a process of slow elucidation through reflection. Unity is achieved, then, in an "a posteriori" manner. A pragmatic process replaces the assertive nature of the a priori effort. Yoder believes, however, that violence remains in the search for unity regardless of which way it is achieved. Whether the unity is secured on the front or back end it remains a violent enterprise. The erasure of plurality remains in effect; it is either

---

23. Ibid., 89.

24. Yoder, "Meaning After Babble: With Jeffrey Stout Beyond Relativism," 125–39. The story of Babel is located in the eleventh chapter of Genesis. The story tells about a community's work to build a tower that will afford them security from their surroundings. According to the story, God visits this community and sees the work they have accomplished. God does not approve of their construction and confuses the people by causing them to speak in different languages. This event effectively scatters the people because they are no longer able to clearly understand one another.

25. Stout, *Ethics After Babel*.

enforced prior to the project or as the project moves forward. Stout's work ends up reinstalling this violence because it remains committed to articulating uniformity, even if it is from the backdoor. Violence and force are the nature of such tower building and the use of philosophical materials to glean a unifying discourse easily becomes a part of that violent enterprise.

Revolutionary Subordination

The primary location of this concept is found in Yoder's famous book *The Politics of Jesus*.[26] This book divides into two large sections which align themselves with Yoder's two main goals: to demonstrate, on biblical grounds, the political nature of the stories of Jesus and to explicate the implications of that political vision for Christian identity and discipleship. Revolutionary subordination is found in the second part of the book. It is, therefore, a part of the implications drawn from the political aspects of the Gospel accounts. The concept of revolutionary subordination is a form or pattern of behavior derived from the political significance of the Jesus story. Yoder draws this concept from the various moral codes found throughout the New Testament records. These codes are located mostly in the Pauline corpus, but can also be found in 1st Peter. New Testament scholarship has labeled these codes with the German word "Haustafeln," which roughly translates to "household precepts."[27] Revolutionary subordination is an ethical practice that calls Christians to subordinate themselves to the relational structures of their existence. According to Yoder, this approach seeks to express the radical political implications of Jesus' life, death and resurrection in non-violent terms – "the voluntary subjection of the church is understood as a witness to the world."[28]

The purpose of Yoder's employment of this concept is twofold. First, Yoder wants to demonstrate, contrary to the consensus of New Testament scholarship, that the aim of these codes is not borrowed from the Roman and Greek culture. The purposes of the *Haustafeln*[29] are derived from Jesus' life, death and resurrection. They are an expression of Jesus' political vision.

26. Yoder, *Politics of Jesus*, 162–92.
27. Ibid., 162.
28. Ibid., 185.
29. The German word signaling the "table codes" or rules governing relational structures within 1st century existence; these codes are located in a number of places throughout the New Testament literature.

These codes demonstrate the efforts of early Christians to think through the implications of that vision for their daily lives. The second purpose is the delineation of a proper engagement with one's surrounding context. These codes propose a proper form of interaction between the relations of wives and husbands, children and parents, and slaves and masters that keep in step with the example of Jesus.

New Testament scholarship, according to Yoder, has monopolized the Christian interpretive tradition of the haustafeln. They have instituted the idea that it is borrowed from external sources (the context of Greek and Roman life) rather than deriving from early Christian reflection. Yoder presents the work of Martin Dibelius as a typical example of this perspective. According to Dibelius, early Christians were not equipped to deal with issues associated with ordinary life because the teachings of Jesus and Paul were too focused on the forthcoming kingdom of God.[30] For Dibelius, then, early Christians were forced to draw on other sources because all that Jesus and Paul had left for them was how to live in the short term. The delayed return of Christ created a new set of challenges for the emerging Christian community, to which it did not immediately have answers.

Yoder's first task, then, is to tell an alternate story regarding these codes. He begins by placing the codes of the New Testament alongside of those found in the wider society of the first century. When these codes are placed side by side Yoder is able to illuminate the important differences between them. In fact, Yoder designates eight crucial differences.[31] Taken together, this array of variations helps lend support to his claim that the codes do not borrow from the wider culture. Yoder believes, instead, that they are demonstrative of the creative initiative of the early Christians. The differences provide validation for the counter story because they show a disregard for the aims and purposes of the codes from Greek and Roman life. Through these differences he is able to demonstrate that the basis of the consensus interpretation is built on the adoption of a particular portrayal of the nature of early Christianity. New Testament scholars like Dibelius believe that these codes are borrowed because they are already convinced that Jesus did not have anything to say for discipleship during the delay of his return.

Yoder's rereading of these codes illuminates the "revolutionary" character embedded in their directives. These characteristics not only separate

---

30. Yoder, *Politics of Jesus*, 164–65.
31. Ibid., 169–79.

the codes from those of Greek and Roman life, but also illuminate the direct correlation between the life and teachings of Jesus with the early Christian community. The pattern of behavior demanded by these codes proved, according to Yoder, that the early Christians were quite prepared for the ethical quandaries presented by a delayed return. They indicate a tactic for engaging one's political context, within that delay, without jeopardizing Christian identity. Revolutionary subordination, then, is a pattern of behavior directed toward the relational structures of existence. This behavior expresses one's association with Jesus and the community that has sprung up from his teachings and life. Christians were expected to live in this manner whether Christ returned the next day or thousands of years later.

Yoder notes three aspects of this teaching that not only differentiates it from its context, but helps to fill out its revolutionary character. First, the codes recognize the dignity and worth of the "inferior" person of the relational dynamic. They offer a robust subjectivity to those persons normally judged as inferior. The codes grant to the "inferior" person of the relationship the moral dignity to choose. They do not assume that this is the case, but explicitly invite the person to participate. This amounts to identifying "(t)he *subordinate* person in the social order . . . *as a moral agent*."[32] This evaluation of the "subordinate person" as a moral agent is lacking from those "borrowed" cultural codes. It also indicates that the early Christian community was willing to make all persons within that community capable of wielding moral agency. The second feature is that these codes called on everyone to practice subordination. No one was exempt from the practice of subordination. In other words, this call to subordinate oneself to the ethical obligations of his/her present relationships was a call for one to exercise personal moral responsibility by aligning oneself under that relational structure. It is a call to willingly wield the moral agency one is granted rather than to just accept things because one happens to have been born a certain type of person. The call to subordination, according to Yoder, indicates that these persons were beginning to experience freedom at levels they had never experienced before. Freedom had to be a part of the Christian experience in order for the Christian communities to articulate proper channels for its development. The codes were implemented in order to help filter the deployment of one's freedom in a manner worthy of the example of Jesus. The net effect was to pattern one's freedom in terms of non-violence. Finally, the codes not only call on the "inferior" person to

32. Ibid., 171.

subordinate him/herself but also the "dominant" partner of that relationship. Yoder believes that this reciprocal aspect of the household codes calls into question the normative order of society. Early Christian communities, against the grain of their current societal structures, took the idea of subordination a step further and charged the "dominant" person of those relationships to also subordinate him/herself. These three elements demonstrate that the household codes are not only different from the codes drawn from the wider world but that this difference derives from an alternative cosmology. Yoder argues that Jesus' political vision is the only possibility for the development of a posture like revolutionary subordination.

The Politics of Jesus: The Cross of Christ as Method and Practice

Yoder's methodology and his articulation of revolutionary subordination are directly related to his conception of Christian discipleship. The political vision embedded in the story of Jesus is the backbone of that discipleship: to follow Jesus means to model his political vision through visible means. This link between discipleship and Jesus' politics is captured in one of Yoder's earliest documents: *Discipleship as Political Responsibility*.[33] Within this little treatise Yoder begins his lifelong endeavor to articulate the relationship between discipleship and political responsibility. Political responsibility for the Christian, according to Yoder, is expressed when the Christian models the political vision of Jesus. Yoder's methodological approach (or lack of one) and his description of revolutionary subordination are extensions of this deeper claim. They are derivative from this vision.

One of Yoder's comments in this work helps to concretely declare the link between discipleship and political responsibility, pointing to Jesus' cross as the exemplification of that link. "It is the consistent assumption of the New Testament that Jesus lives on in the church, Christ's body, and that this becomes visible where the church follows Jesus in innocent suffering."[34] Christian discipleship is described here as a means of expressing the life of Jesus. The link with political responsibility is forged in Yoder's claim that this communal embodiment must be "visible;" i.e., Christians are called to model Jesus to the ever-watching world. Alongside of this linkage, however,

33. Yoder, *Discipleship as Political Responsibility*. The two essays that make up this work were originally given, in German, at conferences during the year 1957.
34. Ibid., 58.

is Yoder's declaration that the shape of this embodiment is located in Jesus' crucifixion; i.e., his "innocent suffering." Yoder believes that the cross of Jesus stands as the central component for comprehending the aim and character of Jesus' political vision. Everything, according to Yoder, points to Jesus' acceptance of the way of the cross and this acceptance becomes the crucial distinctive mark of the politics of Jesus.

"Innocent suffering," however, is a loaded term for Yoder. He argues both in *Discipleship as Political Responsibility* and *The Politics of Jesus*[35] that the cross should not be understood as a blanket symbol for all types of suffering. Yoder believes that the "pastoral care" interpretation of the cross, whereby Jesus' death becomes a symbol for someone who might be suffering unexpectedly from a serious sickness, misconstrues the nature and reach of the crucifixion by failing to recognize its political ramifications. Jesus' crucifixion is wholly a political death; it is not a random or purposeless event.[36] The cross is, according to Yoder, the clash between two competing political visions. Jesus refusal to play by a certain set of rules is an essential factor for prompting its occurrence. The political vision, which is described in this comment as "innocent suffering," is brought about by Jesus' unwillingness to compromise his mission or pattern of behavior. The cross is a punishment given to a person who challenges the prevailing social order. Jesus' death occurs because Jesus seeks to implement an alternative political order that undermines the status quo. This death is the effort of the one political order to silence the other.

This competition between political visions is articulated most clearly in the final chapter of Yoder's *Politics*. This piece contains Yoder's most vivid and lucid account of Jesus' crucifixion. He argues that the dominant strategy for engaging the wider world, both within and without the Christian tradition, has been the effort to locate that one aspect of existence whereby the whole of history can be located and driven.[37] This emphasis on trying to figure out the modus operandi of human history is basically an attempt to reduce all questions to a question of effectiveness. Once this mechanism has been located it can justify any and all action.[38] This particular political vision operates under the assumption that the most effective way to move history is the right way, regardless of the collateral damage that might occur.

35. Yoder, *Politics of Jesus*.
36. Ibid., 129.
37. Ibid., 228–33.
38. Ibid., 229.

Yoder articulates some general points which call this strategy into question, but it is his articulation of the cross as the radical alternative to this strategy which remains crucial for Christians. According to Yoder, Jesus' acceptance of the cross indicates a different orientation with regard to the world because it radically opposes the persuasive sense of getting control of history. Yoder's Jesus rejects this mode and risks being made the sacrificial lamb of this thinking. "Jesus was so faithful to the enemy love of God that it cost him all his effectiveness; he gave up every handle on history."[39] Both the way of effectiveness and the way of the cross are political orientations; i.e. each demonstrates a relationship to power and its proper use. The way of effectiveness, according to Yoder, seizes the opportunity to wield political power in order to bring about the greatest good. The way of the cross, however, is to give up on effectiveness in order to maintain the way of love. This pattern of behavior is especially apparent in the effort to love one's enemy. The crucifixion is the result of a clash between these competing agendas. This means that the Christian community is called to model Jesus' faithfulness by modeling his acceptance of the cross.

Discipleship, then, is the effort to reproduce the fundamental reorientation to existence that Jesus exemplifies. The cross of Jesus is the foundational exemplar of this orientation. Revolutionary subordination and Yoder's methodology embody this political vision. They are an outworking of the patterns of reasoning that this newly described orientation provides. Violently overthrowing one's oppressor or intellectually silencing one's conversational partner derives from the political strategy which places effectiveness over faithfulness. Yoder's methodology and revolutionary subordination are the embodiments of the cross and the rejection of coercive power.

Locations: Methodology and Revolutionary Subordination in Yoder's Thought

Charting Yoder's methodological approach is quite easy. One is hard pressed to locate a moment where Yoder is not being conversational, committed to the biblical record and wary of philosophical materials. Yoder's preference for the essay format for his publications stands as a testament to this conversational style. His unwillingness to write a comprehensive systematic presentation of his thought also highlights this conversational

39. Ibid., 233.

style. The conversational approach dominates Yoder's work and the amount of evidence to prove this case is quite ample.

In the same way that one easily detects Yoder's conversational style, one can locate Yoder's reliance on the biblical record for his work. His posthumously published collection of essays, *To Hear The Word*,[40] is dedicated to mapping out his strategic use of the Bible. At every turn Yoder's work is an effort to reacquaint Christian thinkers with the fecundity of the biblical record. *The Politics of Jesus* exemplifies this by centering its thesis, that Jesus had a political vision, on the biblical accounts. One is hard pressed not to see this argument explicitly carried throughout the bulk of his work. Yoder always made the effort to show how what he was arguing for had a direct relationship to the Bible.

His reticence toward the use of philosophical categories, however, is something that his later writings contain in a more prominent way. This is not to say that it does not exist in his earlier works, but the later writings often contain a more sustained and reasoned argument detailing the dangers of such materials. Of course, his use of the Bible as the primary source for Christian theological and ethical reflection contains an implicit demotion, if not rejection, of philosophical insights. These early writings do, however, also have other indications of Yoder's wariness. He often critiqued biblical scholars for approaching the biblical record with an interpretive grid which told them what it would say before they even had to read the texts. The characterization of Jesus as nonpolitical creates an interpretive grid through which one is unable to see alternative ways of reading certain texts. This placement of the interpretive grid prior to reading the text fails to achieve Yoder's notion of a "naïve"[41] reading of the text. Revolutionary subordination is a significant manifestation of this issue.

The most prevalent interpretation of the household codes was that the earliest Christians borrowed them from Stoicism because they were ill-prepared to develop their own moral ideas. Yoder's problem is not that Christians might have borrowed them (although he does not think that this was the case). He is concerned that this idea is based not on a reading of the text, but on an interpretive framework founded on the notion that the earliest Christians were bereft of any ability to draw their own moral norms from the example of Jesus. Many scholars believe that Christians

---

40. Yoder, *To Hear The Word*.

41. Yoder's idea here is that "naïve" indicates a fresh reading free from such interpretive grids.

were forced, with the delay of the parousia, to look elsewhere for those norms. The idea that Christians borrowed these codes from Stoicism is founded on the presupposition that the Jesus story had no political vision to guide the ethical reflection of the earliest Christians. The parallels with Stoicism are found, according to Yoder, only after one is already committed to finding them there. The use of philosophical categories for setting up the discourse prior to the actual conversation ends up eliminating the possibility of real conversation. After methodology has its say the only thing left to do is to determine where each interlocutor stands. Conversation is closed off because the work is already accomplished in the development of the overarching methodological framework. Yoder's approach was always to allow a text or an interlocutor the space to speak. For Yoder, the turn to philosophical materials was a way of extinguishing all conversation.

Locating discussions of his methodological approach were quite easy, but finding his employment of revolutionary subordination takes a more thorough search. Yoder never explicitly returns to this conception, but one can locate its thematic logic within several points of his work. Three examples help to demonstrate his continued commitment to this form of engagement. First, Yoder discusses Paul's treatment of the issues regarding women and slavery in *The Christian Witness to the State*.[42] His comment is instructive for how revolutionary subordination is to be understood in the larger context of the Christian tradition.

> Over against the tendency toward hierarchical structures of authority in pagan society, there is within the Christian church an egalitarian thrust which casts light beyond the borders of the church. *The church does not begin directly by attacking the social structures of pagan society*; in fact, the Apostle Paul has frequently been reproached for his social conservatism, as evidenced in his willingness to accept for the time being the institution of slavery and the subordination of women.[43]

Yoder proposes that revolutionary subordination is an egalitarian behavior. Yoder argues that Paul's references to slaves and women were not meant to support "the hierarchical structures of authority in pagan society." The reason Paul appears to side with the status quo of those structures is his unwillingness to implement improper forms of conduct to change them. Revolutionary subordination is a proper form of engagement because it

---

42. Yoder, *Christian Witness to the State*.
43. Ibid., 18. Italics mine.

does not violently oppose the norms of the larger social context. It teaches mutual respect and it models an alternative social experience that can rival the ordinary relational experience of that larger context. Revolutionary subordination engages the wider world through faithfulness to the example of Christ. This produces an egalitarian alternative to the oppressive social structures of society.

The second instance occurs in his article "A People in the World."[44] Yoder argues that Christians already have the necessary tools to communicate their message to the wider world. Their commitment to Jesus, which is exemplified in their actions as well as their speech, carries within it the power to speak to their wider social context. To demonstrate this point Yoder argues that certain "marks" or practices of the Christian community can and do communicate patterns for contemporary living, which can be employed by Christians and non-Christians alike.[45] Yoder employs the suffering service of 1Peter 2.18 as an example of suffering that communicates a message. The Petrine reference is part of the Haustafeln codes. Suffering service is combined with the command for submission (which occurs in 1 Peter 3.1–12). This suffering embedded in the concept of revolutionary subordination models the message of Jesus' crucifixion, especially the willingness to follow God at any cost.[46] Here revolutionary subordination is held up as an example of both what it means to follow Christ and the cost of that following. The egalitarian thrust of revolutionary subordination is exemplified by the "meaningful assuming of the cost of nonconformed obedience."[47] The wife, husband and slave are not obedient to their partner because of a "resigned" commitment to accept things as they are,[48] but because they have freely chosen to follow the God exemplified by Jesus' teaching and life. Yoder sees the Christian's willingness to accept his/her situation not as a validation of that state of affairs, but rather as a validation of Jesus' orientation against coercive forms of power. The Christian is "patient"[49] in order to witness to Jesus' fundamental rejection of coercive

---

44. Yoder, "A People in the World" in *Royal Priesthood*, 65–101.
45. Ibid., 75–89. Yoder will lengthen this idea in his book *Body Politics*.
46. Ibid., 87.
47. Ibid., 86.
48. Ibid., 86.
49. Yoder is famous for making patience into an important term for Christian ethics; the key article for this argument is his "Patience as Method in Moral Reasoning: Is an Ethic of Discipleship 'Absolute'" in *Wisdom of the Cross*, 24–42.

forms of power. The hope is that this act of discipleship will foster an awareness of radical alternatives to coercive power. Jesus' crucifixion serves as a model for alternative forms for engaging socio-political issues.

The third example does not contain an explicit reference to revolutionary subordination, but it articulates the logic behind this concept. Yoder's article "The Christian Case for Democracy,"[50] identifies a pattern of living within the call for subordination. Subordination is an attempt to dislodge the Christian community from the use of violent power while simultaneously witnessing to alternative forms of community. Under the subheading "Gospel Realism,"[51] Yoder claims that current forms of political power are manifestations of human rebellion (in terms of the fall of Adam and Eve). Yoder draws his understanding from Luke's account of Jesus' discussion of Roman authority structures.[52] According to Yoder, Jesus is merely describing the fact of dominion with regard to human political structures. Jesus is neither confirming nor denying the reality that such structures "lord it over" one another; he is merely stating the patterns associated with those forms of political power. Jesus' identification of those structures is significant because he is helping his disciples to locate themselves outside of that paradigm. In other words, Jesus "is not a cynic, he does not say that the claims are false. He does not, like a modern Marxist, brush them aside as ideological window dressing," instead, Jesus is making the case that his followers are playing "a different ethical game." Yoder believes that Luke's account produces a general view of the relationship between Christian communities and their sociopolitical contexts; namely, the normative procedure of fallen human political power, which is described as domination and the use of beneficent language to legitimate that domination, will not be the mark of Christians. Revolutionary subordination is one practice that embodies this alternative form of political existence. The rejection of the standards and procedures of normative human political power is exemplified in the Christian's unwillingness to violently overthrow the relational structures of his/her current experience. Subordination, however, is not to be understood as a complacent acceptance of things as they are, it is, rather, a decisive choice to operate under a different set of rules which grants value to the other person even if that person is an enemy. The cycle of domina-

---

50. John Howard Yoder, "The Christian Case for Democracy" in *Priestly Kingdom*, 151–71.

51. Ibid., 155–59.

52. Luke 22.24–27.

tion is broken not by bringing forth a stronger form of political power, but by changing how one plays the game. Revolutionary subordination is one aspect of this radical alternative.

Conclusion

Yoder's approach and his articulation of practices like revolutionary subordination are windows into his deeper understanding of the aim and character of the political vision of Jesus. These elements demonstrate the interesting and controversial features of Yoder's work. On the one hand, Yoder's return to the Bible and his conversational style are unusual and make for interesting reading. On the other hand, it clearly places him in a strange relation to the wider discussions within Christian theological and ethical reflection. His unwavering commitment to the biblical record and its consequences for philosophical insights make his work difficult to attach to these wider discussions, not to mention how revolutionary subordination appears out of step with current calls for liberation and justice. Nevertheless, his willingness to hold lively discussions with just war theorists rather than rejecting them outright and his gracious acceptance of another's point of view, even, in some cases, to the point of not providing a corrective response demonstrate the appeal of his thought. It at least demands a closer inspection of his critics and the attempts of his supporters to account for these idiosyncrasies; it calls for a way of rearticulating these deeper issues in a language that will help to clarify his thought without attaching him to ideas and concepts he would have clearly rejected.

chapter two

A Sectarian Thinker?

Critical Reflections and Questions Concerning John Howard Yoder's Thought

Introduction

JOHN HOWARD YODER'S WORK has been generally well received. Most commentators continue to view his *Politics of Jesus* as one of the most lucid accounts of Christian pacifism. There can be no doubt that this particular work will continue to serve as a staple for courses in Christian ethics, especially for sections on war and peace. These positive remarks, however, contain a negative side. Because Yoder was so articulate when it came to pacifism he is often limited to that articulation. Few, then, have sought to go beyond this limitation. Comments from John Donahue's review of Yoder's *Politics of Jesus* show this simultaneously positive and negative perspective.

> Though much of what Y. [Yoder] says is not new, his work represents a consistent and well articulated NT theology of pacifism which is not passivism. There are, however, serious exegetical difficulties with the work . . . . In the hermeneutical sphere, while criticizing Bultmann for proclaiming only a formal ethic of obedience, Y. himself is in danger of proclaiming a formal ethic of suffering, where pacifistic suffering is self-justifying. Such a view leaves large questions of the relation of Jesus' ministry to complex ethical issues unanswerable.[1]

1. Donahue, "*The Politics of Jesus*," 180.

Donahue recognizes the lucidity of Yoder's account while also noting the difficulty of implementing his work. Donahue typifies the response to Yoder's work in that he affirms its merits while simultaneously arguing for its inability to deliver what it promises. Donahue's charge that Yoder's account is "formal" plays off the idea that Yoder presents an overly optimistic perspective that cannot be implemented in "complex ethical issues." In the end, Yoder's work is interesting and well-argued but not suitable for serious Christian reflection.

Mark Nation's biography of Yoder describes this characterization from the perspective of a supporter of Yoder's work. According to Nation, there are three types of responses to Yoder's work: radical implementation, general acceptance, and affirmation without deep engagement.[2] The first two responses make the effort to broaden their perspective of Yoder's work. They have moved beyond the idea that Yoder was interested only to provide a clear analysis of Christian pacifism. The third posture is akin to Donahue's comments. The limitation that Yoder is merely a spokesperson for pacifism and that his work is not capable of implementation is founded on an insufficient engagement with his work. Nation believes that there was much more to Yoder's work. For Nation, Yoder was not merely articulating the contours of the Anabaptist heritage. He was rather attempting to open up dialogues with other Christian perspectives so that all forms of Christianity (including his own) could work toward a more faithful representation of the Christian tradition. Nation believes that comments from people like Donahue are founded on the faulty idea that Yoder's thought is merely an Anabaptist novelty. It might work for isolated groups like the Amish and Mennonites, but on a larger scale it could not properly cope with the ethical aspects of contemporary experience.

Craig Carter's account of Yoder echoes Nation's reading. According to Carter, one of the chief reasons for mischaracterizing Yoder's work is that he was

> Pigeonholed as a representative of one (extreme) type of Christianity that needs to have a place at the ecumenical discussion table (to show how open we are) but that is known in advance to have the specific function of representing the extreme end of the spectrum and therefore not a viable option for mainstream Christianity. In other words, the value of the Mennonite/Anabaptist (or radical reformation or believer's church) perspective that Yoder is

---

2. Nation, *John Howard Yoder*, xviii–xix.

taken to represent is not that it can be taken seriously as a debating partner but that it defines a sectarian extreme that rounds out the spectrum of positions under consideration.[3]

Carter characterizes most commentators as having a twofold response: it is positively affirmed for its ability to clearly articulate one of the extreme perspectives within the Christian tradition while it is simultaneously denounced for its inability to actually have an impact on the contemporary moral experience beyond isolated communities of faith. Nation and Carter propose that two issues are at work in these responses to Yoder. First, they have read very little of Yoder's corpus. For instance, Donahue's characterization that Yoder's pacifism is only "formal" fails to account for his earlier work *The Original Revolution* where Yoder makes the effort to demonstrate the viability of his perspective for actual ethical concerns.[4] They have largely limited their engagement with Yoder to his *Politics of Jesus*. The second issue is that these commentators have wrongfully attributed a typological slant onto Yoder's materials. This has the effect of funneling the interpretation of his work into a certain direction. Carter calls this "pigeonholing." Yoder is characterized solely as a "sectarian" thinker. This undermines the attempt to overcome the first issue because no matter how much Yoder one reads it will all be read as deriving from and supporting this "sectarian" perspective. Carter and Nation believe that Yoder's work is misidentified because of these two factors. They argue that too often criticisms and support of Yoder's work fails to untangle itself from these mischaracterizations.

Interestingly, the problem associated with Yoder's detractors can be also brought to bear on his supporters. One can argue that a similar kind of blindness occurs when a supporter of Yoder reduces the criticisms of Yoder's perspective to a use of the sectarian charge. In other words, these supporters claim that Yoder's critics fail to fully appreciate the depth of his work and that this failure is drawn from their insistence to read him as a sectarian thinker, but, in a like manner, it is possible that Yoder's supporters mischaracterize these critics. It would be, then, unfair to merely write off their criticisms without a closer inspection. One may find that some of the critical points raised by these thinkers can and do have some potency. The need to better understand one's interlocutor is a blade that cuts both ways.

---

3. Carter, *Politics of the Cross*, 19.

4. Yoder, *Original Revolution*; one could also include his *Christian Witness to the State*.

The purpose of this chapter is to provide a closer examination of some of the criticisms raised against Yoder's work. Like Carter and Nation, I believe that Yoder's work contains ways of responding to these criticisms, but unlike them I am also interested in locating more accurately the contours of the claims that these critics make against Yoder. This chapter will begin by briefly describing the "sectarian" label. This is necessary for gaining a clearer account of its origins and application to Yoder's work. Next, the chapter will take up the criticisms of three thinkers: James Gustafson, A. James Reimer, and Elisabeth Schüssler Fiorenza. These thinkers develop lines of critique that expose some of the weaknesses of Yoder's material. Although they partly rely on the "sectarian" charge to make their critiques, they also illuminate important and unique limitations in his thought. Recognizing these contributions is necessary for demonstrating the need to recast Yoder's work through a referential philosophical framework. The chapter will end with a brief discussion of Yoder's own responses to these criticisms. Yoder defended himself against their claims, but these defenses did not always clear up the confusion. This section of the chapter points toward to the next by illuminating the partial nature of Yoder's responses. This chapter lays the groundwork for mounting a more complete answer to his critics.

The Sectarian Charge

The description of Yoder's work as "sectarian" was, according to Stanley Hauerwas, one of the quickest ways of making Yoder "testy."[5] Yet Yoder never seemed to be able to quite shake off this characterization of his work.[6] He spent a great deal of time and effort to demonstrate that his work did not move in that direction. One of the ways that he sought to challenge this accusation was by reminding his critics that the term was originally a description and not a judgment. Yoder knew better than many of his critics that this term did not originate with its contemporary pejorative aspects. He realized that the term originated merely as a descriptive tool. The idea

---

5. Nation, *John Howard Yoder*, 1.

6. Yoder, *For The Nations*. The introduction to this book, which is also one of the last published in his lifetime, continues to wrangle with the charge that Yoder operated out of a "sectarian" perspective. The nature of the essays collected in this book should be considered as yet another attempt by Yoder to dissuade his critics from characterizing him in this way.

that the contours of this position should be viewed negatively arose at a later time and place.

Ernst Troeltsch, in his important two volume work *The Social Teaching of the Christian Churches*,[7] is considered to be one of the first to employ this term. Troeltsch's work was an effort to delineate and categorize the history of ideas within the Christian perspective. He sought to better understand the dichotomy between the dogmatic postulations of that tradition and the changing landscape of human experience. He hoped to demonstrate the interplay between these opposing points of contact. One of the elements of his study was the illumination and description of the "sect" type. The development of this idea was only to describe a particular pattern of behavior within one portion of Christian history. Troeltsch was not interested in judging whether this facet of the Christian tradition was positive or negative.[8]

This comment illuminates the contours of the "sect" type.

> In general, the following are their characteristic features: lay Christianity, personal achievement in ethics and religion, the radical fellowship of love, religious equality and brotherly love, indifference towards the authority of the State and the ruling classes, dislike of technical law and of the oath, the separation of the religious life from the economic struggle by means of the ideal of poverty and frugality, or occasionally in a charity which becomes communism, the directness of the personal religious relationship, criticism of official spiritual guides and theologians, the appeal to the New Testament and to the Primitive church…the sect, on the other hand, appeals to the ever new common performance of the moral demands, which, at bottom, are founded only upon the Law and the example of Christ.[9]

Two important traits stand out from the description above. First, the sect is characterized by the radical attempt to implement a literal obedience to the love of Christ. This means that these Christians were willing to

---

7. Troeltsch, *Social Teaching of the Christian Churches*, 2 vols.

8. Franklin H. Littell notes that for Troeltsch the Church type and the Sect type were both important aspects of the Christian tradition and that neither one should be viewed as more important than the other. Quoting from Troeltsch, Littell points out that Troeltsch saw "both types" as "a logical result of the Gospel;" in other words, the idea that the sect type was a mistake is not to be found in Troeltsch's materials. Littell, "Church and Sect," 262–76 (263).

9. Troeltsch, *Social Teaching of the Christian Churches*, vol. I, 336.

curb their economic and social practices to reflect this commitment. They refused to compromise this demand of love in order to better fit in their particular social situation. One of the results from this commitment was an unwillingness to utilize violence or coercion to accomplish their goals. The turn to violence was to disregard Jesus' command to love. Another facet of this effort to remain faithful to that command was the desire of these Christians to separate from the larger societal context. These Christians sought to isolate themselves in order to enhance their ability to remain faithful to that command. Second, these Christians placed a staunch priority on the biblical record as the primary source for their theological and moral reasoning. They tended to do what the text indicated. This meant that the Christian is able to hear the command of God directly through the biblical record and he/she does not need a mediator to help articulate this message.

These two aspects are the elements involved in the move from a purely descriptive to a more negative assessment. Paul Deats, in an article about Protestants and pacifism, offers an illuminative description of this development.[10] With regard to the pacifist tendencies of such communities, Deats argues that many outside observers believe that these communities fail to offer any real substantive component for political and social discourse. The criticisms launched against the communities are described in this way.

> It is seen as *legalistic*—supplying answers before questions are put; *simplistic*—assuming the state can turn directly from violence, with love seen as too easy a possibility in history; *isolationist* and *neutralist* in facing international problems of order and justice— and thus *irresponsible*.[11]

Deats highlights four key criticisms aimed at the sectarian perspective. These aspects are given a negative assessment because of what it produces: irresponsibility. Whether it is standing by while someone is being harmed or foolishly trying to disarm a dangerous gunman by telling him that you love him, the pacifist impulse of the "sect" type community fails to take account of reality thereby jeopardizing the lives of all who are involved.

The unswerving commitment to love at all costs and the unwillingness to consider information gleaned from outside sources pushes these communities out of the political sphere. The problems raised here are most acute when a thinker, like Yoder, attempts to implement these various elements

---

10. Deats, "Protestant Social Ethics and Pacifism," 75–92.
11. Ibid., 78.

into the larger societal context. This attempt to integrate these components is considered irresponsible and dangerous. As the "sect" type moves to engage its wider world its characteristics cause that outside context to deem it irresponsible. The sectarian label moves from describing certain types of communities to a negative evaluation of these communities.

The charge of "sectarianism," then, is no longer an objective description of a particular community. The term now bears a negative assessment of those it describes. The critiques leveled at Yoder's work carry echoes of this charge within them. One can certainly trace portions of their questions back to this source. Even with these traces, it would be a mistake to reduce them to that charge. There is more to these critiques than the mere assertion that Yoder's work is sectarian and therefore unusable. Taking a closer look at the contours of the critiques raised by these thinkers enables one to better understand how to go about mounting an answer from within Yoder's work. Closely examining these critiques paves the way for abandoning the point counterpoint dialectic of the sectarian debate. The effort to maintain the importance and relevance of Yoder's work hinges on being clear about its limitations. The detailed examination of these critiques pushes past the blind spots of the sectarian charge—the reception of Yoder's work is changed by paying closer attention to what his critics are saying.

James Gustafson: A Question of Methodology

The most prominent of the three critics to be examined is James Gustafson. He is viewed as one of the premier Christian ethicists of the 20th century. His work is known throughout the world and his students are also prolific scholars in their own right.[12] His relationship to John Howard Yoder's work is an interesting story. On the one hand, Gustafson's remarks regarding Yoder's work are often viewed by Yoder's supporters as negative. Craig Carter argues that Gustafson's material on Yoder is a prime example of the narrowed reading. According to Carter, Gustafson's comments on Yoder are a cursory glance rather than actual engagement. Gustafson is able to provide some "grudging respect," but he could "write his *magnum opus* on Christian theological ethics in the 1980's without refuting Yoder's position in detail."[13] On the other hand, however, this characterization of Gustafson's view of Yoder is counterbalanced by the interesting story that Gustafson

12. Lisa Sowle Cahill and Stanley Hauerwas are two examples.
13. Carter, *Politics of the Cross*, 20.

was instrumental in helping to achieve the publication of Yoder's essay regarding Karl Barth's views on war.[14] The fact that Gustafson made this effort to see Yoder's work published indicates, in contrast to Carter's point, something more substantial than "grudging respect." Writing him off as merely pigeon-holing Yoder's work without attending to his argument fails to give Gustafson a fair hearing.[15]

There are basically two central locations where Gustafson directly engages Yoder's work. The immediate reading of the passages in question appears to substantiate the idea that Gustafson does not give Yoder a fair reading (thereby supporting Carter's assessment). A closer inspection, however, reveals that Gustafson's comments regarding Yoder take place within a larger argument. The recognition of this larger context helps to show Gustafson's deeper engagement with Yoder. The two locations are found in Gustafson's *Protestant and Roman Catholic Ethics* and *Ethics from a Theocentric Perspective*.[16] Although his comments appear brief, Gustafson places Yoder's work into the context of his larger questions and concerns. These larger concerns and questions provide the necessary depth associated with Gustafson's comments about Yoder.

The overarching context is generally aimed toward concerns about one's methodological starting point. In *Protestant and Roman Catholic Ethics* Gustafson articulates what he believes ought to be the launching pad for work in Christian ethics. His comments regarding Yoder take place in relation to his proposed starting point. The second set of comments, found in his *Theocentric Ethics*, is concerned with delineating the weaknesses of other starting points; namely, that much of Christian theological and moral reasoning has originated from an anthropocentric base. The trajectory of these critiques is directed at Yoder's methodology. Yoder's unswerving commitment to the biblical record, in all cases, as the primary source for Christian theological and moral reasoning as well as his unwillingness to

---

14. Mark Thiessen Nation, in his work *John Howard Yoder: Mennonite Patience, Evangelical Witness, Catholic Convictions*, relates that James Gustafson oversaw the publication of this book and most likely helped to get the book purchased by the bookstore at Yale Divinity School (54). Interestingly, Nation also remarks that this is where Stanley Hauerwas got his introduction to Yoder's work. The book in question by Yoder is his article "Karl Barth and Christian Pacifism" which was later published in *Karl Barth and the Problem of War*.

15. Carter, *Politics of the Cross*, 19.

16. Gustafson, *Protestant and Roman Catholic Ethics* and *Ethics From a Theocentric Perspective*, vol. 1.

A Sectarian Thinker?

translate his understanding of Christianity into philosophical terms falls into the purview of Gustafson's concerns. The reasons for Gustafson's rejection of Yoder are found in this larger concern of methodology and this section will illuminate that concern.

Beginning with the passages in *Protestant and Roman Catholic Ethics*, one can see that Gustafson values the contribution of philosophical work for helping the causes of the Christian tradition. Gustafson views philosophy as an essential partner for communicating the good news of the Christian faith. According to Gustafson, one of the main tasks of Christian theological work is to locate and articulate a philosophical foundation or starting point whereby one can better collect and effectively disseminate theological data.[17] The purpose of this philosophical edifice is to help the project to remain faithful to its identity as a Christian work while simultaneously connecting to contemporary concerns of modern experience. The overriding justification of the search for a proper philosophical foundation is the necessity for Christians to share their message beyond the borders of the ecclesial community. Wherever Christians fall with respect to questions of revelation or inspiration they must employ "extratheological and extrabiblical"[18] arguments to support their positions. These arguments are necessary for proclaiming their message. Christians, then, are already in the business of employing means and conceptual frameworks that originate outside of the parameters of their tradition. Gustafson merely notes that the value of Christian theological and ethical reflection should be measured by its relationship to that reality.

Gustafson indicates that the link between the Christian message and a philosophical base is necessary for producing a fruitful theological project. Gustafson draws out three characteristics of such a project.

> Thus Protestant theological ethics and Catholic moral theology currently share a serious quest, namely, for a philosophical foundation for Christian ethical thought and Christian moral activity which takes the Christian tradition seriously, which provides a common ground with nonreligious persons and communities with other religions, and which has openness to historic changes and to personalistic values without becoming utterly relativistic.[19]

---

17. Gustafson, *Protestant and Roman Catholic Ethics*, 60–61.
18. Ibid., 63.
19. Ibid., 62.

The three aims are: maintaining identity, communicating with non-Christians, and openness to new data, both in form and content. Philosophy is, then, both helpful and necessary for formulating a successful theological project. It is especially instrumental for accomplishing the second and third aims. Philosophy offers Christians the ability to communicate with outsiders as well as a second language for incorporating data that exceeds the descriptive base of the scriptural records.

Gustafson views Yoder's work as moving away from these aims. In particular, he states that Yoder's focus is to eschew "a general philosophic justification for the morality of the distinctive historic tradition."[20] Yoder's primary aim is to articulate the Christian tradition in terms of the life of Jesus with "the biblical materials providing its norm and content."[21] Due to this focus, Yoder's work places a priority on the maintenance of the community's identity. We have seen that Yoder is concerned with attempts to articulate a universal "philosophic justification." For him, this will lead the Christian tradition further from its identity. The essential aspect of his work, then, is a prioritization of the biblical record above other types of sources. Gustafson makes the stronger claim that Yoder's focus is to move the Christian tradition away from "that moral and social responsibility" which "requires the Christian community to be something other than 'a faithful witnessing minority.'"[22] Yoder's claim that "(f)idelity to Jesus is the moral principle of the church; not rational concepts of justice or of the common good"[23] undermines his theological contribution. It is, in a word, a withdrawal from some inherent responsibilities of the Christian tradition.

Yoder's work, then, rejects the importance of locating and articulating a philosophical framework thereby also rejecting the need to make Christianity appealing to persons outside of the tradition. Certainly, it fulfills the necessary requirement to maintain its identity, but it accomplishes this feat through the exclusion of these other important tasks. Placing the biblical record as the foremost source for discerning social issues forces Yoder's project to neglect these other aims. Gustafson perceives this strategy as amounting to the view that "does not believe that the historical developments in which the churches find themselves require a basic reconsideration

---

20. Ibid., 66.
21. Ibid., 67.
22. Ibid.
23. Ibid.

of their ethics."[24] Yoder's work fails to account for the real problem of distance between contemporary experience and that experience of the earliest Christians. Contemporary experience is subordinated, if not altogether eliminated, to the biblical record. This strategy is, according to Gustafson, akin to avoiding the question. Yoder's desire to place the biblical record above all other possible sources, even though it is done in terms other than "fundamentalism,"[25] ends up damaging his work. Yoder's failure to answer questions in terms set by Gustafson doom him to a well-articulated call for something like a sectarian withdrawal: the main trajectory of the Christian tradition is to be a "faithful witnessing minority."

Gustafson's second set of comments further this critique by delineating negative features associated with methodologies that refuse to embrace all three of the aims above. The successful theological project can no longer be evaluated only by its fruitfulness it must also be viewed in terms of how it avoids the pitfalls of a false sense of certainty and anthropocentric thinking. These comments indicate that a healthy theological project is one that also cultivates ambiguity and a theocentric perspective. Gustafson states that

> The limits of human capacities to control all consequences of our interventions into the natural and historical processes of life, while being decreased in some arenas, nonetheless remain, and as a result action involves risks.[26]

"Risks" are an essential part of any theological project and the attempt to overlook or dispel this reality diminishes the project. The horizon of Gustafson's claim here goes well beyond the Christian tradition. Risk is the condition of human existence. Because of this reality the Christian tradition cannot fool itself into thinking that this is a nonissue. The generation of a false sense of certainty is a detrimental perspective. Theological projects that fail to account for this reality make foolish promises. The overlooking of the fundamental human experience of risk keeps the project from delivering on those promises.

The ignorance of the risky nature of human experience further develops into a faulty line of reasoning, which Gustafson labels as anthropocentrism.

---

24. Ibid.

25. Gustafson is quick to note that Yoder's strategy should not be viewed in parallel to the strategies of fundamentalists. The key distinction, according to Gustafson, is that Yoder does not tie his understanding of the text to "theories of inspiration." Ibid. n. 5.

26. Gustafson, *Ethics from a Theocentric Perspective*, 1:7.

The Trace of the Face in the Politics of Jesus

The basic thrust of this thinking is to place the human being as the centerpiece of one's project. This state of affairs, that is a blindness to the risky nature of human existence, leads to the effort to undervalue the nature of risk. This, then, leads to an unhealthy effort to overcome the limited nature of human existence whereby a community doubles its efforts to eliminate the risky aspect of existence. The result, especially for the Christian tradition, is that all of its activities are transformed into "instrumental" devices which seek to attain "subjective temporal human ends."[27] The religious tradition, with all of its resources and materials, is called "to assure people that whatever seems to bring them happiness is what they ought to do, and whatever impediments there are to that aspiration…have no significantly binding force."[28] In this way, the religious tradition becomes a kind of narcotic that aids in covering up the ambiguity imposed by the risky nature of human existence. The Christian faith is turned into a coping mechanism that seeks to carry on a fairy tale existence where its adherents are promised a certainty that no tradition can provide. Christianity is abducted for a person's personal battle with uncertainty. It fails to prepare its adherents for the difficult journey of existence by making promises that blind them to the true travails of life. Gustafson argues, "(t)he temptation of religion is always to put the Deity and the forces of religious piety in the service of the immediate needs and desires of individuals, small groups, and societies."[29] Anthropocentrism occurs as a result of this unwillingness to take ambiguity seriously. Christian theological projects that foster such ends are not only weaker, but are dangerous as well.

The cure for this situation is to start from the position of ambiguity. In other words, the tonic is not to avoid it, but to plunge headfirst into it. The acceptance of risk is, for Gustafson, the acceptance of human finitude. This realization of one's finitude brings about the theocentric starting point because one recognizes that he/she is no longer the center of the universe. The recognition of ambiguity develops the understanding that the universe is no longer viewable as solely for the service of human existence; it has its own agendas and purposes which can and do conflict with those that are human. A religious tradition that can start from here is a religious tradition that achieves a theocentric starting point. The Christian theological project, if it is to be theocentric, must not seek to overcome the risky nature of

27. Ibid., 18.
28. Ibid.
29. Ibid., 25.

human existence and thereby install an anthropomorphic tradition. These two dangers—a false certainty and anthropocentrism—are now linked to the objectives above; not only must a theological project seek to maintain its identity, converse with outsiders, and take into account its shifting context it is also required to foster uncertainty and a God-centered universe. Gustafson believes that Yoder's work fails to fulfill these goals. He argues that Yoder seeks to offer a false sense of certainty which leads to the danger of turning the Christian tradition into an instrumental project for maintaining an anthropocentric starting point.

Yoder's commitment to the biblical record and his wariness of philosophical work leaves his project open to Gustafson's concerns. This turn back to the Bible makes Yoder's work untenable because it fails to account for the necessity of detailing a "philosophical base"[30] and it fails to nurture a healthy uncertainty and God-centered universe. The Bible becomes the source of the certainty because it is viewed as the only wellspring for Christian theological and moral reflection. Yoder's methodological starting points are interesting, as Gustafson is quick to note, but his approach invites the dangers mentioned above. Yoder's turn to the Bible ends up supporting the notion that the Bible contains all of life's answers. This, in turn, leads to the viewpoint that Christian practices, God, and the Bible are instruments for human experience—they are made to serve only those needs. Yoder's strategy fails to appreciate these important questions and thereby eliminates itself for being a genuinely effective theological project.

James Reimer:
An Undernourished Picture of the Biblical Record

Reimer's critique is important for two reasons. First, unlike the other authors gathered here, Reimer is also a Mennonite. Reimer's critique, then, is also based out of a common heritage. In fact, Reimer admits to both his desire to align himself with Yoder while simultaneously distancing himself. Part of what makes Reimer's work valuable is his ability to illustrate depth and broadness within the Mennonite heritage. It is common for many thinkers to reduce that heritage solely to the work of Yoder, but Reimer's work indicates that this is an incorrect way to read Yoder and the Mennonite tradition.

---

30. Gustafson, *Protestant and Roman Catholic Ethics*, 60ff.

The second reason is Reimer's interconnection with Gustafson's work. The fact that Reimer is concerned with Yoder's methodological work echoes elements within Gustafson's critique. Reimer, like Gustafson, is concerned that Yoder's work is limited by his rejection of philosophy. The main difference, however, is that Gustafson's invitation is for Yoder to use philosophy in order to make Christianity more coherent to a wider world whereas for Reimer he is interested in the use of philosophy to help make Christianity more articulate to itself. Gustafson's aim was to help Christianity in its effort to articulate itself to outsiders, but Reimer's concerns are with how Yoder's lack of philosophy leads to an undernourished self-portrait.

It would be unfair to try to reduce the complexity of Reimer's critique to one statement, but his comments here set the stage for discerning the contours of his critique. "It always seemed to me that Yoder was 'right' in a limited sphere of life and knowledge, but that his thought could not provide a comprehensive foundation for many other areas of reality and human existence—music and the arts, to give just one example."[31] The emphasis here is on providing a theological framework for helping Christians understand the nature of human existence. The implicit question here is whether Yoder's work helps the Christian tradition to better understand the natural expressions of human existence, like music and art. Reimer's point is that Yoder's work is limited to a different kind of discourse and that it would harm these communities of faith because it ill-equips them for entertaining the questions embedded in these pursuits. What does the *Politics of Jesus* have to say about establishing and enjoying Beethoven's Ninth Symphony?

Reimer points to Yoder's hermeneutic as a chief cause for rendering his work useless regarding these fundamental aspects of the Christian experience. Yoder's use of the "Constantinian"[32] typology too often defines such activities as falling outside of the parameters of faithfulness. Essentially, Reimer believes that Yoder's limitations derive from the way in which he avoids certain ways of thinking because they are too easily influenced by

31. Reimer, "Theological Orthodoxy and Jewish Christianity: A Personal Tribute to John Howard Yoder" in *Mennonites and Classical Theology*, 304. This article was originally published in the *Festschrift* for Yoder: Hauerwas et al., *Wisdom of the Cross*, 430–48.

32. Constantinianism is an important and common theme throughout Yoder's work; however, there are two important articles that help to establish its contours: "The Otherness of the Church" in *Royal Priesthood*, 53–64 and "The Constantinian Sources of Western Social Ethics" in *Priestly Kingdom*, 135–47. The basic thrust of this perspective is that Christians begin to commit themselves to governing the world as well as maintaining the life of the community. This new direction forces them to have to ask questions in terms of effectiveness rather than in terms of faithfulness to Jesus.

the "Constantinian" framework. The problem with music and art is that it utilizes alternative methodological approaches that are more interested in running empires than being faithful to God. Yoder's division of history into two approaches, obeying Jesus or being effective, is garnered by rereading the history of Christianity in terms of the Constantinian mistake; being faithful or unfaithful is attached to where one positions oneself with regard to this event. This division, according to Reimer, gets inserted into Yoder's hermeneutical strategy wherein he is now justified in sweeping aside large aspects of the Christian theological tradition because it is too closely associated with that perspective.

Reimer finds this problem based largely in Yoder's rejection of the Classical Christian theological tradition.[33] Reimer argues that Yoder defines these materials as a "postbiblical *Hellenistic* development" and "a departure from (the) biblical narrative into metaphysical-ontological thinking."[34] For Yoder, one element of the Constantinian mistake is the acceptance and implementation of the Western philosophical tradition as an equal, and sometimes superior, source for Christian theological and moral reasoning.

Yoder's assessment that the biblical record is written in terms of the "Hebraic" mindset and that philosophy is developed from "Hellenism" further solidifies his division of history. The Hebraic mode is characterized by Yoder, according to Reimer, as a "prophetic-eschatological" approach.[35] This approach reads the biblical record "in social-political terms." The Hellenist position, however, is described as a "priestly sacramental" approach. Reimer argues that this latter description is associated with the "sacramental, mystical, cultic, metaphysical, and ontological" modes of Christian history, which are present in the doctrinal/creedal formulations of the early church periods.[36] The crux of this division is that any effort to reflect on the deeper points of the biblical account and Christian experience are viewed as harmful. Yoder's hermeneutic strategy here, according to Reimer, posits that discipleship, based on the "Hellenist" materials, becomes an intellectual rather than a social commitment. The advent of this "Hellenistic"

---

33. Reimer describes this material as being closely related with the doctrinal/creedal formulations of the early Christian churches.

34. Reimer, "Theological Orthodoxy and Jewish Christianity: A Personal Tribute to John Howard Yoder" in *Mennonites and Classical Theology*, 307.

35. Ibid., 306.

36. Ibid.

approach transforms Christianity into a set of propositions to be believed rather than a life to be lived.

One of the founding arguments that Yoder employs to support his reading is the diasporic experience of 1st century Judaism. According to Reimer, Yoder views the synagogue as an early form of the "Free Church tradition."[37] The parallel aspect is decentralization of power invoked by the creation of a worship center beyond the temple's parameters. In other words, Yoder reads the development of the synagogue as a counter or antagonistic community toward the second temple. In his estimation, the synagogue acts as a form of "Hebraic" thinking whereas the second temple is cast as deeply infused with "Hellenism." This reading of Jewish history confirms his suspicion and rejection of the more speculative aspects of the Western philosophical tradition. The line of demarcation between faithfulness and unfaithfulness run along this counter center of worship and continue into Christianity's future agreement with Rome.

Reimer contests this view as failing to take account of actual history. Yoder's desire to read a Constantinian framework onto Jewish history is part and parcel of his larger inability to take seriously all of the tools necessary for making such hermeneutical judgments. The idea that Jewish synagogues were diametrically opposed to the second temple is just erroneous. This does not mean that there weren't tensions between the two religious institutions, but an outright rejection is an over-exaggeration. It is a faulty rereading of Israel's history. The suspicions that Yoder carries regarding the Western philosophical tradition are read back into 1st century Judaism. Judaism is portrayed as an example of this contrast between the Hebraic and Hellenist modes. The problem, though, is that this finely laid distinction is just not accurate; it does not and cannot comprehensively account for 1st century Jewish religious experience.

Yoder's suspicion of the doctrinal/creedal formulations of the early church is founded on this idea that they are developed out of this Hellenized Constantinian perspective. This helps to explain why Yoder spends very little time discussing important Christian theologians like Augustine and Aquinas. He views these thinkers as participating in the Constantinian problem. Reimer's conclusion, then, is that Yoder's perspective limits Christianity. The idea that one could speak comprehensively about Christian experience in Yoderian terms is hard to believe. It is Yoder's perspective which is ultimately flawed, especially its basis in a faulty rereading of

37. Ibid., 309ff.

Christian history. Reimer's point is not that Yoder's quest for a faithful life is wrong, but that to exclude all of the resources available for continuing that quest is futile. Reimer believes that Yoder's overuse of the Constantinian framework ends up positioning the Christian tradition in an antagonistic posture regarding human existence. A comprehensive view of Christian experience would need to include the insights of the philosophical tradition. This would not only help to articulate its experience to outsiders, but also for comprehending its own identity. Yoder's work is limited both in its trajectory to the outsider and to Christian adherents. The suspicion of philosophy leads to an underdeveloped self-understanding. Christianity becomes a stranger unto itself.

Elisabeth Schüssler Fiorenza: The Forgotten Quest for Justice and Equality

Schüssler Fiorenza's remarks criticize Yoder's work on both methodological and substantive grounds. Her comments echo the sentiment of both Gustafson and Reimer with regard to Yoder's use of the biblical record, but she is also concerned with the type of behaviors or practices Yoder furnishes from his methodological approach. In this way, Schüssler Fiorenza provides a concrete example of Yoder's limitations through a criticism of his notion of revolutionary subordination.

The bulk of her comments regarding Yoder are located in her book *Bread Not Stone: The Challenge of Feminist Biblical Interpretation*.[38] A central theme of this book is the delineation of gender issues and its relation to biblical interpretation. Interestingly, Schüssler Fiorenza, like Yoder, argues that the biblical record contains the moral reflections of the early Christian communities. This means that she also desires to keep the Bible as a theological and moral authority for Christian communities. The difference, however, is that Schüssler Fiorenza finds this record laced with concerns and negative connotations, especially for women. She argues that "the Bible and its subsequent interpretations are sources for both liberation and oppression."[39] The implication from this claim is that it would be foolish to attempt a "straightforward" reading of the biblical record. Such a reading is bound to overlook some of these more negative aspects. Yoder's notion of revolutionary subordination, then, is an example of this methodological

38. Fiorenza, *Bread Not Stone*.
39. Ibid., 67.

problem of overlooking those areas of patriarchy and other forms of oppression.

The household codes are prime examples of this continuing link with oppressive patterns of thought.[40] Yoder's effort to demonstrate a clear line of continuity between the liberating messages of Jesus and passages like the household codes are more about maintaining biblical authority than about proclaiming liberty. Schüssler Fiorenza is concerned with Yoder's articulation of revolutionary subordination because it appears to reinscribe a kind of conservatism; it sides with the importance of maintaining a unified biblical record over against the plight of women and slaves. This is a classic example of neglecting justice and equality for maintaining the status quo. The point here is that Yoder is oblivious to what these codes are calling for and that his attempts to recast them as a "voluntary subordination" to a governing order does nothing to minimize their underlying oppression. Schüssler Fiorenza takes issue with Yoder's methodological approach, as did Reimer and Gustafson, by viewing his work in terms of an uninformed hermeneutic. His articulation of revolutionary subordination fails to take seriously the underlying themes of oppression. This is caused by his effort to read the texts "straightforwardly."

Schüssler Fiorenza's discussion about the cultural influences that support these codes serves as strong support for her critique. Like Yoder, Schüssler Fiorenza argues that these codes are not directly borrowed from Stoicism, but are, instead, more reminiscent of Aristotelian thinking.[41] Her link with Aristotle is a break with Yoder's claim that the lack of Stoic origins proves a direct link to early Christian thought. The idea that these codes call for a reciprocal subordination does not prove their Christian origins. The Aristotelian accounts carry a similar line of thinking and still end up reinforcing a patriarchal bias. These texts are an instantiation of the kind of negative cultural baggage that other biblical texts seek to overcome. Yoder has not discovered a single theme of liberation, but has rather stumbled onto a moment where the liberating message of Jesus has been stifled by the insistence of maintaining the status quo. Yoder's hermeneutic here, then, is nothing more than a way of reinstituting the very same kind of conservatism that helped to get these texts into the record in the first place.

Alongside of this methodological critique, however, is also a critique of the substance of Yoder's concept. Schüssler Fiorenza argues that Yoder's

40. Ibid., 70–92.
41. Ibid., 72ff.

work carries within it a call to "accept things as they are"[42]—women are called to take their experience as it comes rather than actively seeking to make it better. Quoting from Yoder, Schüssler Fiorenza notes Yoder's disdain for "the sweeping, doctrinaire egalitarianism of our culture" by noting his characterization of it as being "demonic" and "uncharitable."[43] These comments, with their charges of demonism and lack of love, indicate this undermining of the impetus for change. Basically, the attempt to bring about change is akin to being unfaithful; it is an affront to the will of God.

This problem is heightened by Yoder's effort to tie Jesus' suffering to the practice of revolutionary subordination.[44] This builds a symbolic paradigm wherein suffering service is described in terms of subordination thereby eliminating the idea that suffering can be put into service for changing unjust structures. This suffering paradigm is not only dangerous because it heads off any attempt to overcome an unjust setting, but it is also dangerous because it can very easily become an ideological instrument used to maintain the plight of oppressed people groups. Suffering service gets inscribed onto those that are suffering. Sufferers, especially unjust sufferers, are viewed as participating in the declaration of the truth that suffering is faithfulness. The effort to change that state of affairs, then, is a demonic act.

Schüssler Fiorenza criticizes Yoder's methodological return to the biblical record continuing the trend begun in Gustafson and working through Reimer. She also points out a dangerous aspect of this approach in that it undercuts the impetus to seek change. Genuine moments of injustice and oppression are at best allowed to continue and at worst strengthened by the call to suffer. Yoder's approach and his development of the practice of revolutionary subordination are deemed problematic. He is unaware of the hermeneutical nuances within the biblical record and he is insensitive to the plight of oppressed persons.

Yoder's Response

This chapter began with the recognition that it was unfair to merely reduce Yoder's work to the charge of "sectarianism." This same charge, though, also applied to reducing Yoder's critics to merely espousing a "sectarian"

42. Ibid., 82–83.
43. Ibid., 83.
44. Ibid., 82.

argument against his work. The examination of these three critics demonstrates the superficial nature of that latter claim. Their work indicates deeper limitations with Yoder's materials. One issue is how Yoder's work limits the Christian tradition. The problem is not that Yoder advocates a withdrawal from ethical issues in order to maintain a pristine identity, which is akin to sectarian forms of withdrawal, but that he fails to advocate a conception of Christianity that fully utilizes its resources for dealing with contemporary concerns. Yoder's work ill-equips the Christian tradition for theological and moral reflection.

Yoder spent a great deal of time working against the idea that he was sectarian. Certainly, some of his efforts toward disarming this characterization were rightly conceived, but it did not always clearly address the issues raised against him. Sometimes he refused outright to directly address the issues raised against him. Yoder offered an explanation of this refusal in a posthumously published essay.

> It is not simple for an author to deal with this kind of critical response which rejects what had been argued without dealing with the textual and historical basis on which the argument rests. One can argue with the non-biblical assumptions which the critic holds and which have kept him from reading the text straightforwardly without being conscious that they are non-biblical. But it is difficult to lift up and argue with the unavowed philosophy of one's own culture.[45]

The basic thrust of Yoder's point is that his critics failed to raise issues against the contours of the argument he offered. They bypassed his reading of the biblical record and proceeded to argue their fundamental assumptions. The problem, then, is not with Yoder's argument but the critics' way of reading.

The curious aspect of this point is his recognition of their critique and his unwillingness to directly engage the assumptions underlying it. Yoder's approach to these issues was to "simply go back yet again to the text, to read it again, still more modestly."[46] Yoder believed that he should reread the biblical accounts, more patiently and modestly, in order to restate the

---

45. Yoder, "There is a Whole New World:" The Apostle's Apology Revisited" in *To Hear The Word*, 9–10.

46. Ibid., 10. The background for these two quotes is Yoder's *Politics of Jesus*. Yoder was reacting to the critical remarks raised against that book when he authored these particular statements.

argument he was trying to make. He hoped that through this rereading of those accounts his critics would come to realize their faulty assumptions. Rather than offering a direct challenge to those assumptions, he believed that his reading of the biblical record would illuminate the flawed nature of those suppositions.

This refusal to engage his critics in their own terms has helped to fuel the impasse. There are, however, other moments, albeit few, where he has taken a more direct approach to his critics. In fact Yoder has offered three direct responses to the critics in this chapter: twice to Gustafson and once to Schüssler Fiorenza.[47] Each of these more direct responses demonstrate both that Yoder was capable of providing the kind of response that he refused to give in the aforementioned statements and that they still leave some elements for further development.

Yoder's most detailed response to Gustafson is his paper given at the symposium honoring Gustafson's *Ethics From a Theocentric Perspective*.[48] Yoder argues that Gustafson's work fails to demonstrate why Christians should consider his position. This failure presents itself in two distinct ways. First, Gustafson fails to show why Christians are to no longer be bound by certain parts of the tradition. Yoder believes that Gustafson belittles or bypasses certain elements of the Christians tradition (e.g., the incarnation) without presenting his argument for leaving them behind. The second element is Gustafson's positing of scientific data or human reason over against biblical revelation as the primary source for Christian ethical discourse. In each case Yoder believes that Gustafson's contention for these points of view is predicated on mere whim. Yoder argues that Gustafson does not take up the task of charting out why Christians should follow his conjectures. Yoder's problem with his approach is that Gustafson radically alters the identity of the Christian tradition without providing reasons, from within the tradition itself, for setting aside those markers. The historical integral marks of the Christian community can and should be challenged, but Gustafson does not provide a valid reason for making those changes.

---

47. Although Yoder's work does not directly deal with Reimer's critiques, Reimer tells of an interesting story where he and Yoder made a lengthy road trip together. Reimer was able to voice some of his concerns, but all that Yoder responded with was a statement that he was impressed with how closely Reimer had read his materials.

48. The materials of this symposium are contained in Harlan R. Beckley and Charles M. Swezey's *James M. Gustafson's Theocentric Ethics*. Yoder's response is contained on pages 63–94.

The problem with this approach is that it does not address Gustafson's claims regarding Yoder's work. There is an indirect link in that the issue of identity is a primary aspect of the conversation, but it is articulated in a point-counterpoint procedure. Yoder only seems interested in showing that Gustafson's work argues from a faulty basis. He appears to only be interested in bringing to light the deeper assumptions of Gustafson's material rather than to explicitly deny their validity. Gustafson could go back and rewrite *Theocentric Ethics* in a way that would include the kind of argument Yoder seeks. The end result is that one is no closer to finding a solution to what Gustafson raises regarding Yoder's work.

The second response to Gustafson is carried out along the same lines as the one above except that Yoder articulates more clearly why Gustafson's relegation of community identification is problematic and why it is possible for the Christian community to present itself to the wider world without having to relinquish its chief identity markers. Yoder's essay, "On Not Being Ashamed of the Gospel,"[49] argues that Gustafson's dichotomy between "authenticity" and "intelligibility" is a "null-sum game."[50] Yoder asserts that Gustafson's claim that Christians must sacrifice portions of their identity in order to remain intelligible to outsiders is false. He also claims that there is a pattern whereby one can both make sense and maintain one's identity. Yoder illuminates that behind Gustafson's construal of this problem is the hidden assumption that there is some kind of universal non-particular way of arguing. This "public" forum, which is often associated with human reason, stands over against the particularity of traditions like Christianity and forces this choice. Yoder's critique of this position is that there is no such thing—all forms of human reason and public forums are nothing more than other particularities. To frame the debate on the basis of a choice between intelligibility and authenticity is to falsely assume that some kind of universal medium exists. This critical perspective points back to Yoder's previous response to Gustafson because it echoes his call for an explanation for abandoning the community's identity markers. What Yoder wants for Gustafson to show is the contours of this non-particular time and place—to demonstrate that the choice between authenticity and intelligibility is a fact of reality.

---

49. Yoder, "On Not Being Ashamed of the Gospel: Particularity, Pluralism, and Validation," 285–300.

50. Ibid., 288.

A Sectarian Thinker?

Yoder moves from this critique to make the point that even though the world is engulfed in particularity it does not mean that communication cannot occur. In fact he argues that certain New Testament texts already point to a way of both maintaining the identity markers while simultaneously communicating its truth outside of traditional lines. The opening passage of John's Gospel serves as one of his examples. According to Yoder, the early Christians articulated Jesus in terms of the Greek "logos" as a means to make their claims intelligible to the wider world. They borrowed this term from that context and put it to work as a means of communicating with outsiders. The key in this maneuver is that they did not allow that terminology to set limits on their understanding of Jesus, but rather spun it around so that their understanding of Jesus could redefine what logos could mean. This is how they were able to maintain their identity as Christians. The content of their faith could be shared through the languages of the numerous cultures surrounding them. Yet, in doing so, they did not allow the translation to ultimately undermine their own content. The logos idea became a bridge whereby Christians and non-Christians could communicate without either side having to abandon its identity: intelligibility occurs in the midst of identity. For Yoder, then, the New Testament serves as a model for future attempts by Christians to articulate what and who they are without abandoning their particularity.

These two elements serve as a positive response to Gustafson's points. Yoder shows that the notion of a non-particular place and time does not exist, which then points to the possibility of seeing parts of the New Testament as models for articulating one's claims across numerous lines of particularity. There is also a more negative element to Yoder's article. He not only believes that Gustafson's work is founded on a faulty basis, but he is also concerned that Gustafson's effort is intertwined with dangerous games of power. Yoder believes that "the hunger for validation is a hunger for power."[51] The contest between authenticity and intelligibility carries within in it a grasping for control. Yoder highlights that this effort is more complex than the mere choice between maintaining one's identity and making oneself intelligible to another. Yoder's comment posits the idea that underlying the effort to demarcate the universal criteria for a discourse is a subtle mode of violence. This effort is violent because it seeks to forcibly make others confirm to its current power structure and language game.

---

51. Ibid., 287.

The Trace of the Face in the Politics of Jesus

These responses to Gustafson begin to lay a base for mounting a fuller argument, but in its present state it only initiates this type of project. Yoder's work here points to some intriguing lines of discussion between himself and Gustafson, but he does not take the time to fully develop his critique of Gustafson's project. The idea that Gustafson's project contains an implicit commitment to violent modes is interesting, but Yoder does not describe in detail how this violence occurs and how it might work itself out. There is only a beginning here.

Turning to Yoder's response to Schüssler Fiorenza one finds a similar state of affairs. Yoder acknowledges Schüssler Fiorenza's critique inside the epilogue attached to the chapter on revolutionary subordination in his second edition of the *Politics of Jesus*.[52] Basically, Yoder attempts to demonstrate that his aims coincide with those of Schüssler Fiorenza. This leads him to try to articulate that revolutionary subordination can serve as a mode for bringing about change to unjust social structures. The problem is that he never fully develops how exactly this practice could engender change. He states very clearly that "the Haustafeln texts project...a tactic for change," but he does not spell out how that change might be effected.[53] His reason for maintaining the practice is because of its interconnection with the political and ethical import of Jesus' crucifixion. It is a tactic founded on Jesus' mode of engaging the powers.[54] The implication of this interconnection is that Yoder is worried, as he thinks the New Testament writers were, about the mode that brings about change. The cross, for Yoder, serves as a model for engaging the powers in terms of God's nonviolent acts. Christians are to express this connection when they engage their socio-political context. Revolutionary subordination seeks change in a way that coincides with Jesus' political vision. There is a subtle indication that Schüssler Fiorenza's call for justice, which rejects the Haustafeln as modes for answering that call, might incur violent modalities disconnected with Jesus' political vision. Again the issue is that Yoder points in a direction but does not fully develop the contours of this direction. All that one can glean from Yoder's work is the beginning of a reply. What Yoder needs to do is to show in a clearer way how revolutionary subordination brings about change and how other forms of liberation are too closely connected with violence. Certainly this serves as one of the chief theses of his *Politics*, but it must be teased

52. Yoder, *Politics of Jesus*, 188–92.
53. Ibid., 192.
54. Ibid., 190; cf. n. 61.

out and transformed into a more comprehensive argument. The reply, like the replies above, are only the beginning—they are seeds yet to be fully cultivated into fruit bearing plants.

Conclusion

One way of thematizing these critical views is to say that Yoder's work fails to offer a comprehensive account of the Christian tradition, which leads to an underdeveloped view of the Christian community. This underdeveloped portrayal is problematic because it limits the capacity of the community to respond to questions of justice and order. Although Yoder's work is interesting, it continues to be an impoverished account of the Christian tradition.

Yoder, of course, defends himself against these charges. He has attempted, throughout his work, to address these challenges. The brief overview of these responses demonstrated that potential answers could be given, but that these particular offerings remain incomplete. Yoder points to what a comprehensive answer would look like, but does not articulate a fully developed option. The incomplete nature of his responses is, in part, formulated through his methodological approach, especially his reticence to offer comprehensive accounts and his suspicion of philosophical categories. This approach creates obstacles toward offering a more complete response. Nevertheless, many of his supporters have begun to work toward developing thorough answers to these critiques. The following chapter takes up some of these efforts.

The critiques offered here demonstrate that it is not enough to say that they derive from a faulty picture of Troeltsch's "sect" type. It will not do to write them off as such and to continue to do business as usual. Yoder's responses, although only partial, point to the possibility of raising counterpoints. The response that is given must not fall into the trap of merely writing these critiques off as deriving from a faulty "sectarian" position, just as those that would critique Yoder must move beyond the idea that he is merely proposing a withdrawal from socio-political issues.

chapter three

Yoder's Rejoinders

Evaluating the Responses of Yoder's Supporters and Their Employment of the Western Philosophical Tradition

Introduction

THE LAST CHAPTER RAISED three issues with Yoder's work: the incapacity and unwillingness to articulate Christianity to a wider audience, a disavowal of large portions of Christian thought and practice, and an inability to articulate clear and workable solutions to problems of injustice. These problems demonstrated a deeper set of concerns than those normally attached to the labeling of Yoder as a sectarian thinker. Yoder's own responses to these concerns initiated partial answers but have not been viewed as fully answering those questions. It would seem that Yoder's methodological approach and his espousal of practices like revolutionary subordination fail to alleviate the concerns of these critics; in the end Yoder's work is judged as failing to quell their concerns. This chapter examines the work of some of Yoder's most competent proponents. Each of these thinkers believes that the lingering concerns with Yoder are largely predicated on a faulty reading of his work. This charge against Yoder's critics is, however, not without its own surprises. Instead of following the route of Yoder, that is to go back and patiently restate the case, these authors place Yoder's work into conversation with thinkers and concepts largely drawn from Western philosophical thought. I believe that this demonstrates a detection of the limitations within Yoder's work as well as a deep desire to see the continued use of his work for contemporary theological and moral reflection. Ultimately, the chapter will argue that these extensions of Yoder are fruitful but only at the cost of undercutting important aims within Yoder's thought. This chapter, then, serves as the bridge for rereading Yoder in terms of Levinas' philosophical work.

The three thinkers to be examined in this chapter are Craig Carter, Stanley Hauerwas, and Chris Huebner. Each author is firmly committed to the value of Yoder's theological and moral reflections. They view their work as decisively rooted in Yoder's aims. I believe that these three authors are especially valuable for two reasons. First, each thinker is viewed as an expert with regard to Yoder's work. Yoder's material has been employed by each one in his own work. This effort to incorporate Yoder's work into their own lends immense credibility to their skills as interpreters of his work. The second reason is that each author extends Yoder's work by placing him into conversation with portions of the Western philosophical tradition. This effort serves as a validation of this project while also illuminating pathways and dangers for undertaking that course. Their restatement of his work in these terms illuminates the possibilities of extending Yoder into areas with which he did not directly discuss. These restatements also offer strong rebuttals of the objections raised by Gustafson, Reimer, and Schüssler Fiorenza. Re-crafting Yoder's work enables these thinkers to mount a counterargument that both illuminates Yoder's aims and demonstrates the mischaracterizations of his work by these critics.

Along with the gains that these thinkers offer there are also costs. As I examine each thinker's work I will also end by pointing out the limits of their efforts. The effort to tie Yoder to a philosophical frame of reference contains the danger of allowing his work to be swallowed up by that frame. In this manner, Yoder's original purposes can be altered or left behind. The effort to align Yoder's work with these various frameworks provides much needed depth to the responses to his critics, but those solutions come at the high price of mischaracterizing Yoder's work. It should be noted that the mischaracterizations are not intentional; Carter, Hauerwas, and Huebner genuinely seek to retain the authenticity of Yoder's work. This chapter will show that their effort is a noble pursuit and should not be abandoned because of these dangers. Their work stands, instead, as a continuing invitation to locate voices from within the Western philosophical tradition that will better carry the dual effort of maintaining the authenticity of Yoder's work and offering a comprehensive response to his critics. Carter, Hauerwas, and

Huebner remain important due to their demonstration of a positive fruitful pattern of interpretation. Their work truly is a bridge for my own because it is in and through the trajectories of these authors that I have discovered the framework for my own approach.

Craig Carter: Yoder's Continuity with Early Classical Christian Orthodoxy

Craig Carter's efforts to rearticulate the work of John Howard Yoder are largely located in his work *The Politics of the Cross*.[1] One of Carter's aims is to show that one can draw a line of continuation between Yoder's contributions and early Christianity. Carter believes that Yoder's work contains important links with thinkers from early Christianity, especially with those after the infamous Constantinian synthesis. Carter seeks to show that Yoder's Christological focus coincides with the Christological insights of those early Christians, especially those of the Nicean and Chalcedonian formulations. This puts Carter's work in a sharp contrast with that of Reimer. Carter argues that Yoder's thought, in contrast to Reimer's findings, embraces the insights of those early Christians and is, therefore, not a starved version of the Christian theological tradition.

Carter's most valuable resource for bolstering his argument is Yoder's posthumously published lectures on theology.[2] Carter contends that a close inspection of this material reveals that Yoder affirmed the creedal formulations of this time period. Carter highlights important citations and arguments that Yoder offers to help solidify his point. He states that Yoder believed the historical actuality of the incarnation. This means, according to Carter, that Yoder was thoroughly committed to both the divinity and humanity of Jesus. The espousal of this theological concept is a dual commitment in that it articulates both the divine condescension and the totality of human existence. This clearly places his thought within the confines of those early Christological formulations.

Carter ties Yoder's perception of the creedal formulations to George Lindbeck's notion of doctrine as a second order language.[3] In other words, Yoder sees these formulations as an important safeguard to the revelatory aspect of the biblical record. They are developed not to replace, but to serve

---

1. Carter, *Politics of the Cross*.
2. Yoder, *Preface to Theology*.
3. Lindbeck, *The Nature of Doctrine*.

that record. They are works of clarification; that is, they clarify and resolve crises of belief that arise as the tradition marches through time and space. Carter examines Yoder's description of the Trinity as an example of this line of reasoning.⁴ For Yoder the Trinity is neither a direct revelation nor simply does it arise from human reason. This means that one doesn't find the concept directly spoken of in the text, but it is also not solely generated from outside of the text. The development of the concept is, rather, an effort to safeguard certain biblical texts which create "an intellectual difficulty." These passages generate confusion regarding the character and nature of Jesus. The conception of the Trinity is implemented, through a dialogical effort between the text and human reason, to maintain a consistent commitment to the teachings of these texts. The idea that Jesus is both divine and human and that God expresses God's self in terms of father, son, and spirit creates tension for the Christian tradition. The Trinity, then, does not replace the scriptural record, but safeguards its message from distorting errors. Yoder believes, then, that creedal formulations are necessary for the health of the Christian tradition, but that they should not replace the reading of the scriptural record.

Carter's description of Yoder's relationship to the creedal elements of the early Christian tradition sets the stage for his rebuttal of Reimer's critique. Carter argues that Reimer mistakenly attributes a radical historicism to Yoder. Through this historicism, Yoder is charged with undermining important conceptions within Christianity thereby abandoning some of the tradition's essential resources. Carter argues that two reasons stand against this charge. First, Reimer's understanding of Yoder's historicism is, according to Carter, wrongly placed. Carter argues that Reimer fails to make a clear distinction between Yoder's understanding of epistemology and ontology. In other words, "he (Reimer) assumes that, because Yoder rejects a foundationalist epistemology, he must not really mean that the gospel is ontologically true."⁵ Reimer believes that Yoder's position rejects the resources which ground the ontological status of the gospel. This claim is founded, according to Carter, on the combination of epistemology and ontology. This faulty combination leads Reimer to miss the aim of Yoder's skepticism. Carter points out that Yoder is skeptical of attempts to generate universal timeless epistemological arguments, but he is not skeptical about the historical actuality of Jesus' birth, life, death and resurrection.

---

4. Carter, *Politics of the Cross*, 118ff.
5. Ibid., 115.

Carter's claim is that Yoder is not wavering about the events of Jesus' life, but that he is doubtful about finding a methodological way of accessing the truths of those events apart from the gospel accounts. This echoes Carter's link between Yoder and Lindbeck. The role of doctrine is to safeguard the texts, not to replace the narratives. Doctrines, then, do not offer ontological proofs of the facts of Jesus, but are aids for guiding the reading and practice of the Christian tradition.

The second issue with Reimer's reading of Yoder is his disagreement with Yoder regarding the role of external resources in the development of Christian theological conceptions of God.[6] Reimer's argues that both the biblical accounts as well as Greek philosophy (Platonic and Aristotelian thought in particular) play a role in helping to determine the contours of the Christian tradition. For him, the creedal formulations are an invitation to undertake this approach. This reading of classical Christian orthodoxy is certainly at odds with Yoder's conception because it embarks on the campaign to exchange the central component of Christian theology from Jesus to philosophical reasoning. The inclusion of contributions from Greek philosophy helps to generate the search for an epistemological foundation for the Christian tradition outside of its christological center; the insights of Plato and Aristotle become central for Christian theological reasoning. This changes the nature of the creedal formulations from guarding the biblical record to opening it to radical distortions.

Carter argues, through the sociopolitical framework that Yoder unveils regarding the inception and promulgation of the creeds, that Reimer's understanding of the purpose of the creeds is too ahistorical and detached from the ontological realities of the Christian tradition. Reimer's conception of classical Christian orthodoxy posits that these formulations attain universal status and enable Christian use of the Greek philosophical tradition. This conception, though, fails to take seriously the historical events that condition their possibility. For Yoder, according to Carter, the development of these formulations was to safeguard the tradition from error and not to broaden its appeal by indicating a universal extrabiblical methodology like human reason. Basically, Yoder's view of the creeds is embedded in the actual historical experience of the early church to remain faithful to the claims of the biblical record. Carter's argument, then, ironically, places the historicist label onto Reimer. Reimer's conception of classical Christian orthodoxy fails to take the historical context seriously. Reimer's effort is not

6. Ibid., 117.

only ahistorical but it is anachronistic. He imposes the modern obsession with articulating Christianity in "universal" terms back onto that time period. For Yoder, "the content of biblical monotheism and the deity of Jesus are protected from a pagan form of monotheism that is incompatible with the incarnation and deity of Jesus Christ."[7] The creedal formulations are not efforts to make Christianity more intelligible to the outside world, but are efforts to maintain its identity as it engages the wider world.

Carter's argument mounts a serious rebuttal of Reimer's assessment of Yoder. Carter demonstrates that Yoder possesses a greater sympathy with the classical orthodoxy of Christianity than Reimer allows. Still, Reimer is not completely wrong in his estimation of the creedal development. It is hard to argue that these early Christian thinkers did not allow Greek philosophy to aid them in their efforts; a cursory reading of the arguments waged at those meetings clearly indicates that such interaction did occur (both on the side of the "heretics" and the "orthodox"). The debate as to whether Yoder's version of the creeds is more accurate than Reimer's exceeds the limits of this paper. Carter's argument demonstrates that one can read Yoder as being tied back to this portion of the Christian tradition and that suffices to demonstrate that it is not accurate to disconnect him from it altogether. The real issue for this project is whether Carter's appropriation of Yoder leads him to misconstrue Yoder's thought. Does Carter's demonstration of the continuity between Yoder and classical Christian orthodoxy end up moving Yoder closer to something he sought to avoid?

The problems associated with Carter's restatement of Yoder are evident in his characterization of ontology. Carter's characterization of ontology describes it as a belief that things are real or that they exist. Ontology, however, is more complex than this. It is also the effort to explicate that existence through some type of comprehensive framework. Carter's portrayal of epistemology appears to encompass this desire to know what exists, but the desire to know and the method by which one will come to know is a better way of distinguishing the split between ontology and epistemology. Ontology contains the desire to know while epistemology embraces the quest for the proper method for satiating the thirst contained in ontology. A better way of stating this difference is that ontological thinking is like a posture or an approach to all that exists while epistemology is the effort to locate the tools for moving forward in that posture. This lack of attention to

---

7. Ibid., 122.

the complexity of ontology is the entry point for viewing Carter's misconstrual of Yoder's work.

The nature of the creedal formulations is more than what Carter argues for in the above discussion. The rub between Carter's reading of Yoder and Reimer's is that Yoder views the creeds as safeguards and not invitations for entertaining other forms of reasoning outside of the biblical accounts. Yoder's hesitancy regarding those formulations is founded on the danger of viewing them as this type of invitation. Carter argued that if one reads the creeds as safeguards, however, one could avoid the temptation to draw from sources outside the Christian tradition while simultaneously affirming those statements of faith. A problem arises when one views the complexity of ontology. Basically, the desire to comprehensively explicate the content of the faith is also an issue embedded in the formulation of these creeds. Yoder's hesitancy is broader than the worry about non-Christian resources.[8] He was also concerned about the effort to develop comprehensive systematic accounts of the Christian perspective.

Yoder was fond of quoting John Robinson, a Puritan pastor, who exclaimed "the Lord has yet more light and truth to break forth from his Holy Word."[9] For Yoder, Robinson's comment signals a posture of openness with regard to the Christian faith. Yoder believed that Christians would still need to rely on God to help them to move into the future. Robinson's quote indicated to Yoder that God still had more to reveal. This is confirmed in his effort to differentiate himself from fundamentalist forms of Christianity.

> What is wrong with fundamentalism is not that it holds too tightly to the text of Scripture (although that is what it thinks it does). It is rather that it canonizes some post-biblical, usually post-Reformation formulation, equating it so nearly with the meaning of Scripture that the claim is tacitly made that the hermeneutic task is done.[10]

The problem with fundamentalists, according to Yoder, is that they believe that they are reading the scriptural texts when they are actually

---

8. I think that Yoder would still argue that this effort to bring about a comprehensive scheme would continue to bolster the reach for non-biblical sources. In this way, the effort to develop a universal picture of Christianity will necessarily utilize non-biblical sources.

9. Quoted in John Howard Yoder's *To Hear the Word*, 10. Yoder does not offer a reference for Robinson's remark.

10. Ibid., 10.

operating with a comprehensive systematic account of their faith. They are reading an interpretation of the faith rather than the biblical record. This means that, for the fundamentalist, the "hermeneutic task is done." No one has to interpret the text, let alone read it, because it has already been reduced to a systematic portrait. These persons are no longer capable of understanding Robinson's quote above. God has spoken and they have calculated and translated that revelation into a comprehensive scheme which provides them with universal propositional truths. Those truths are now the heart of the Christian faith and their congregations are equipped to handle any future experience through them.

The point is that the creedal formulations can also be viewed as supplying the Christian faith with a timeless universal set of truths thereby dissolving the hermeneutical task. Carter's problem is that he fails to take this element into account in his discussion of Yoder's relationship with classical Christian orthodoxy. Travis Kroeker has noticed this problem.[11] Kroeker argues that the nature of Yoder's work is an attempt to explicate the "logic of lordship."[12] This means that Yoder believed that Jesus' lordship did not secure a power base but "dispossesses all other claims to power, wisdom, and goodness."[13] In other words, Yoder's understanding of Christianity is one that sees Jesus and the scriptural accounts disarming claims to power; it unsettles rather than concretizes what one believes. Carter's work is a "betrayal" of Yoder because he relates him to this systematizing reflex. In Kroeker's terms Carter too closely connects Yoder to a Barthian position in that Carter casts Yoder as a full supporter of Barth's effort to pen the *Church Dogmatics*. Kroeker suggests that Yoder's work stands as a profound contrast to that document. He argues that Yoder's hesitancy toward creedal formulations also places him in contrast with efforts to provide systematic accounts of the Christian faith. Yoder failed to write a comprehensive account of his understanding of Christianity and this failure was based in a deliberate choice. Yoder's hesitancy toward the creedal tradition is not only because of the penchant for allowing extrabiblical sources to guide Christian thought and practice, but also because it is an effort to systematize Christianity.

11. Kroeker, "Is A Messianic Political Ethic Possible?: Recent Work by and about John Howard Yoder," 141–74.

12. Ibid., 145. Kroeker draws this idea from Grady Scott Davis' article "Tradition and Truth in Christian Ethics: John Howard Yoder and Bases of Biblical Realism" in *Wisdom of the Cross*, 278–308 (299).

13. Ibid., 145.

Carter offers an important account of Yoder because he helps to broaden Yoder's work to include classical Christian orthodoxy. Carter shows that Reimer's critique only makes sense if one limits the creedal formulations to an invitation to draw from Greek philosophy. The fact that Yoder could view these formulations in Lindbeckian terms facilitates the possibility of reading Yoder in relation to those statements of faith. The problem is that Carter's effort to demonstrate this interconnection ends up misconstruing an important part of Yoder's thought; namely, his resistance to systematic portrayals of Christianity. Carter unwittingly links Yoder to a tradition which seeks to systematize the Christian faith and thereby loses one of the important aspects of Yoder's work. Carter does not distinguish between the acceptance of the practical necessity of creating creedal formulations and the desire to systematize the Christian perspective. He has rightly shown that Yoder's hesitancy toward the creedal formulations is partly based on the inclusion of extrabiblical sources, but it is also founded on a desire to manage and control the Christian faith through the generation of comprehensive frameworks. Carter pushes Yoder into the direction of closing off the hermeneutical task by making his work into a system.

Stanley Hauerwas: Authenticity and Intelligibility

Stanley Hauerwas has almost singlehandedly maintained the importance and relevance of Yoder's work. To be sure, Yoder's work stands the test of time, but there can be no doubt that Hauerwas' championing of it has bolstered its base of receptivity. Hauerwas' contribution to this task goes beyond the mere mention of Yoder. Yoder's work plays a substantial role in Hauerwas' own. This centrality forces Hauerwas' readers, whether supportive or critical, to have to address the insights he borrows from Yoder.[14] Yoder's work serves as a central piece for Hauerwas' aims and one must account for it if one is to properly address him.

Hauerwas provides a brief sketch of his career in the introductory comments of *The Peaceable Kingdom*.[15] This biographical outline offers a glance at the motivations for his work as well as his most important resources. One of the chief motivations for his work has been the desire to chart a course beyond the impasse between the principled and situational

---

14. An excellent example of this reality is Jeffrey Stout's recent book *Democracy and Tradition*.
15. Hauerwas, *Peaceable Kingdom*, xv–xxvi.

approaches to moral reasoning. The problem associated with these approaches was their reliance on a "decision-based" perspective.[16] Each position, although in competition with the other, arose from this conception of morality as a purely decision making affair. According to Hauerwas, this conception of ethics was based on a faulty view of the moral agent. The decision based approach perceives the agent apart from his/her historical reality.[17] Hauerwas, at the suggestion of his then professor James Gustafson, sought to look for this alternative through a moral approach based on character and virtue. This approach to moral reasoning was a better fit because it embraced the fact of one's historical particularity and it did not attempt to locate an ahistorical approach to moral reasoning.

The motivation to locate an alternative to decision-based approaches led Hauerwas to look more closely at a character based approach. This, of course, propelled him to closely read Aristotle and Aquinas. These two thinkers helped to set the questions and aims that Hauerwas would begin to unfold. His reading of their work helped to strengthen his commitment to work toward a more robust vision of rationality. In opposition to the effort to locate rationality outside of the experience and existence of the moral agent, Hauerwas began to find a way of talking about morality that allowed those elements (experience and existence) to fully participate. Moral discourse was to be shaped in terms of the particularities and contingencies of the moral agent rather than through the effort to leave those things behind.

The full development of this turn to character and virtue was aided by two important thinkers: Alasdair MacIntyre and John Howard Yoder. MacIntyre's work was significant for helping Hauerwas to delineate both a more robust critique of ahistorical approaches to morality and a deeper analysis of the contours of a character based approach. One of MacIntyre's positive contributions to Hauerwas was the recognition that all rationality was constituted through a tradition. Hauerwas labeled this constitutive

---

16. Hauerwas, "Situation Ethics, Moral Notions, and Moral Theology" in *Vision and Virtue*, 11–29.

17. At first glance, this would seem to not fit the situational approach to ethics because of its reliance on circumstances for making a decision. The rub, however, is that situational ethics continues to elevate the ideal of the ahistorical moral agent in that he/she is to not allow his/her historical particularities to influence the perception of those circumstances. The emphasis of the "here and now" of the situation stands against what the moral agent could bring to the moral situation; in fact, if the moral agent were to draw from such resources he/she would no longer be making a decision based on the situation.

aspect "narrative."[18] Basically, Hauerwas argued that all forms of rationality are based on some story about the world. This comprehensive story provided both the means and accountability for the rational endeavor. Even the decision based approaches were embedded in a story, albeit a story about how to extricate oneself from such stories. Hauerwas' point was that human activities and experience were contained within larger narratives and that these larger narratives provided the framework for making sense of the nature of those works and their directionality. This conception of rationality, according to Hauerwas, contained important points of contact with MacIntyre's own description of traditions. Virtue and character, which were embedded in the story world of a particular tradition, are an alternative to contemporary efforts to ground moral discourse in an ahistorical framework; it is not that decisions do not play a role in morality, but that they are part and parcel of a larger narrative which helps to formulate the motivations and justifications of those decisions. Hauerwas' insights about this approach were confirmed and expanded by MacIntyre's work.

Hauerwas' work in the area of moral discourse has expanded to include a reconception of the Christian community as one of virtue and character. Again, MacIntyre's work has been invaluable for this effort. *Character and the Christian Life* and *A Community of Character*, two of his earlier works, contain comprehensive arguments for this reconception of the Christian community.[19] Alongside of this redevelopment of Christianity, Hauerwas has also borrowed from MacIntyre the articulation of decision based approaches as faulty and dangerous. One of the main theses in MacIntyre's *After Virtue* is the recognition that contemporary approaches to moral experience are not only flawed, but that they actually end up undermining moral experience altogether.[20] The effort to locate moral norms outside of actual moral experience is detrimental because it fails to provide an account for why one action is preferable to another; it lacks criteria that can help these moral musings from devolving into mere opinion and assertion. This leads MacIntyre to describe contemporary moral discourse as a catastrophe. Hauerwas was able to detect these same problems arising within the Christian tradition. *After Christendom*,[21] a work whose title appears to

---

18. Burrell and Hauerwas, "From System to Story: An Alternative Pattern for Rationality in Ethics" in *Foundations of Ethics and its Relationship to Science: Knowledge, Value and Belief*, Vol. II, 111–52.

19. Hauerwas, *Character and the Christian Life*; *A Community of Character*.

20. MacIntyre, *After Virtue*, 2nd ed.

21. Hauerwas, *After Christendom?*.

coincide with MacIntyre's *After Virtue*, signals an assault on the dangerous liaisons between liberal moral discourse and Christian ethics and theology. The dangers of these encounters is that Christian discourse no longer appears to be aimed at establishing and maintaining Christian communities; instead, they have abandoned those particular aspects which made them distinct so that they might participate in the efforts for constructing a world free of its historical particularities and contingencies. This has resulted in a radical reconstruction of what it means to be Christian. Hauerwas borrows from MacIntyre this critique of liberal approaches to morality to help impede the Christian community from further investing in that pathway. The dangers exposed by MacIntyre are extrapolated by Hauerwas as dangers for the Christian community. Character and virtue are viewed by Hauerwas as the pathway out of this chaos and he has spent a great deal of his time trying to help Christians to understand themselves in this way.

Yoder's work, like MacIntyre's, also contained important insights for Hauerwas' efforts. One of the early problems that Hauerwas ran into trying to articulate the approach derived from character and virtue was its purely formal character. In other words, Hauerwas was adept at describing the contours of the virtuous community, but much weaker on providing its content. Yoder's work, especially his *Politics of Jesus*, helped Hauerwas to fill in the gaps. Yoder's description of Jesus and his political vision, especially his nonviolence, enabled Hauerwas to move past his formalistic accounts of virtue and character. Yoder's work transformed his abstract account into a robust picture of practices and habits predominantly derived from the Christian stories of Jesus.

The other element that Hauerwas has borrowed from Yoder is the stress on Jesus' nonviolence. According to Hauerwas, one of the most important elements for viewing the Christian church as a community of virtue and character is to recognize the importance of peace. Hauerwas' understanding of Yoder's conception of peace is larger than merely refraining from the use of violence. Hauerwas believes that peace, or as he labels it in *The Peaceable Kingdom* "peaceableness," is essential for the community of character and virtue.[22] This significance is rooted in Hauerwas' belief that peaceableness is necessary for maintaining the community's capacity for truthfulness. Truthfulness is important, according to Hauerwas, because it is the only weapon against the human penchant for deceiving itself. This deception covers over human uses of violence to maintain order, but it

---

22. Hauerwas, *Peaceable Kingdom*, 135–51.

constantly needs to be readdressed. Truthfulness is based in peaceableness because honesty about the violent tendencies can only be brought about when a person trusts that he/she will not be destroyed for what he/she has done. Peace, then, makes possible the Christian practice of forgiveness because confession is not met with destruction. The other virtues of the community can be achieved because the basis of the community stands firm against the deceptive practices of violence.

Turning now from this brief sketch, we are better suited to view the ways that Hauerwas extends Yoder's work and the role that MacIntyre plays for developing this extension. The clearest place to view this is located in Gustafson's criticisms of Yoder's work. Reflecting back, Yoder responded to Gustafson by trying to articulate an alternative approach that could both maintain the authenticity and intelligibility of the Christian community. Yoder argued that the effort to locate a separate medium that could arbitrate between the various particular histories and languages of people was a grasping for power. Yoder indicated that the effort to locate this ahistorical starting point veiled deeper plays of power; for Yoder this endeavor was an attempt to control as well as to aid communication. The problem was that Yoder did not fully develop this critical view. Hauerwas, however, has made this critical issue one of his main theses. Hauerwas' work has placed him in direct contact with Gustafson; in fact, Gustafson names Hauerwas as one of the premier theological thinkers pushing a "sectarian" agenda.[23] Gustafson's basic thesis is that Hauerwas overemphasizes the identity of the Christian tradition which results in disabling its ability to clearly articulate itself for contemporary issues: Hauerwas sacrifices intelligibility for the sake of authenticity. Hauerwas' response to this criticism is not difficult to locate. Although he wrote a direct response to Gustafson, one can still view this concern throughout his corpus.[24] Hauerwas responds by noting that Gustafson's use of the "sectarian" judgment is too simplistic and that one of the real rubs between himself and Gustafson stands on the issue of prioritizing the resources of Christian moral and theological reasoning. The problem is not that Hauerwas actively calls the Christian church to withdraw into isolated enclaves, but that Hauerwas' positioning of revelation over against other sources like human reason undermines the ability of the

---

23. Gustafson, "The Sectarian Temptation: Reflections on Theology, the Church, and the University" in *Moral Discernment in the Christian Life: Essays in Theological Ethics*, 142–54.

24. Hauerwas, "Why the 'Sectarian Temptation' is a Misrepresentation: A Response to James Gustafson" in *Hauerwas Reader*, 90–110.

Christian church to be relevant to the issues confronting the contemporary wider world. Withdrawal seems more like a resulting consequence of this ill-equipped church rather than a forefront mandate.

One of the key points between them is the issue of scientific data. The stress on authenticity fails to prepare the Christian tradition for incorporating the insights gleaned from this resource. Issues like euthanasia, sexuality, and abortion are solved by resorting to ancient paradigms which may no longer be useful due to the advent of recent scientific developments. Hauerwas argues, however, that Gustafson does not take into account the diverse complexity of scientific research. According to Hauerwas, Gustafson fails to ask "which scientific conclusions should be considered and why?"[25] Hauerwas does not seek to derail scientific work. On the contrary, he seeks to show that one always approaches this material from a starting point, including the scientists themselves. Christians can and should interact with scientific research, but they do not have to abandon their Christian heritage in order to do so.

One of the fullest accounts of Hauerwas' critiques of this approach and his solution is located in his Gifford Lectures *With the Grain of the Universe*.[26] The premise of this book is simple: "that natural theology divorced from a full doctrine of God cannot help but distort the character of God and, accordingly, of the world in which we find ourselves."[27] Hauerwas' effort in these lectures is to show that the move to free rationality from its contingencies is problematic and dangerous. It is problematic because it cannot be accomplished and it is dangerous because efforts to do so only end up severely "distorting" identity. These arguments are mounted through the works of Yoder and MacIntyre. Here Hauerwas affirms Yoder's insistence that all Christian theological and ethical reflection must begin with the Christian story within the biblical record: revelation precedes human reason (it is important to note that Hauerwas is not eradicating natural theology, but that it must take place within the confines constructed by the information gathered by revelation). The second element of this focus is the description of the danger contained within this effort to supplant revelation through a stand alone natural theology. This second element, however,

---

25. Ibid., 98. See also Grady Scott Davis' comments in his article "Tradition and Truth in Christian Ethics: John Howard Yoder and the Bases of Biblical Realism" in *Wisdom of the Cross*, 278–305.

26. Hauerwas, *With the Grain of the Universe*.

27. Ibid., 15.

is better articulated in and through the work of MacIntyre. Drawing on MacIntyre's assertion that human rationality can only be rational when it is conceived within the structures and assumptions of an already agreed on tradition, Hauerwas attempts to demonstrate that the Enlightenment project (which is characterized as a tradition-free model of rationality) contains an insidious aspect; namely, it misconstrues the nature of God and undermines the community of Christians through isolation and abandonment of its peculiar identity. This second feature is an extension of Yoder's critique because it more fully develops the danger he originally detected. The combination of Yoder and MacIntyre indicate the erroneous features of a stand-alone natural theology and its inherent dangers.

The import of this is that Gustafson's work is an effort to create a stand-alone natural theology that falsely esteems these extrabiblical sources of data as having overcome the problems of history and location. There is no external way of mediating between competing claims of knowledge; one is always working within the confines of history and location. It will not do to try and live as if such methods of validation existed. Every community must utilize its own resources when it encounters opinions and ideas outside of its boundaries. Hauerwas' response to Gustafson rightly indicates that he gives these other sources of information too much credit. The problem is not that Gustafson desires for Christians to validate their claims, but that he wants them to do it in ways that end up removing their Christian particularity.

Hauerwas extends Yoder's suspicions regarding the effort to translate Christian speech and identity into terms that will be more easily understood by those on the outside of that community. Hauerwas' notion of "witness" indicates an alternative to that effort that allows Christians to maintain their identity while simultaneously engaging their wider societies through their speech and action. These extensions of Yoder, which are partly predicated on the work of Alasdair MacIntyre, appear to line up with Yoder's aims. He rightly understands Yoder's concerns with an approach like Gustafson's and he offers an authentic Yoderian alternative to that approach. The cost of his extension is viewed when one attempts to compare the ecclesiological outcome of their respective work. Hauerwas' portrayal of the Christian community, which is entrenched with his critique of Gustafson, does not adequately match up with Yoder's own view. The type of community that Hauerwas has in mind moves in a direction away from Yoder's conception.

The evidence for this position arises from an unlikely source: Romand Coles. Coles, a professor of political science at Duke University, characterizes Yoder's work as supportive of his effort to articulate "radical democracy."[28] Basically, Coles argues that Yoder's conception of the Christian community, especially the receptive vulnerability it has with outsiders, offers important insights for moving democracy closer to its own aims. This reading of Yoder's work has placed Coles in a position to critique Hauerwas. Coles argues that Hauerwas' combination of Yoder and MacIntyre produces a blind spot to important elements of Yoder's ecclesiology. The centrality of MacIntyre's work forces Yoder's portrayal to conform to it. This results in a loss of some of Yoder's unique contributions.

The overarching problem is that Hauerwas' work lacks the ability to be vulnerable to outsiders. It is only capable of seeing itself as a giver and not a receiver when engaging the wider world.[29] The basis for this thesis is lodged in Coles' critical remarks regarding MacIntyre's work.[30] On the whole, Coles views MacIntyre's work in a very positive light. MacIntyre is viewed as offering a very intriguing position. The problem, however, is that MacIntyre is not always very clear on how a tradition makes internal changes and it is this stultifying element that worries Coles. The nature of this problem is not that MacIntyre has provided a description of encounters that bring change, but that he articulates a "confidence" that can result in moving the community away from vulnerable encounters toward a more defensive posture. Coles believes that Hauerwas' work may contain this lack of reception as well—Yoder is more likely to be open to transformation in the encounter with another whereas Hauerwas seems more concerned to resist what the other person offers.

Coles points to two important elements of Yoder's thought to bolster this opinion. First, Coles recounts Yoder's articulation of a proper understanding of tradition. Coles notes how Yoder's perception of tradition is both a "reaching back" as well as an open vulnerability to future change. In either case, Jesus works as a detotalizing agent in Yoder's thought—not allowing the Christian community to idolize either its past or its present. Yoder's use of a vine over against a tree as the key metaphor for understanding tradition helps to demonstrate this point.[31] The vine demonstrates the

---

28. Coles, "Wild Patience of John Howard Yoder: 'Outsiders' and the 'Otherness of the Church,'" 305–31; Coles, *Beyond Gated Politics: Reflections for the Possibility of Democracy*.

29. Coles, "Wild Patience of John Howard Yoder: 'Outsiders' and the 'Otherness of the Church,'" 307.

30. Coles, *Beyond Gated Politics: Reflections for the Possibility of Democracy*, 79–108.

31. Coles, "Wild Patience of John Howard Yoder: 'Outsiders' and the 'Otherness of

importance of interruption through the activity of pruning. Coles' point is that the truth of Jesus articulated in Christian communities is "always a finite historical incarnation."[32] This state of affairs is located both externally and internally—the claims of any particular Christian community do not supersede the reality of historical incarnation. The Christian church is always particular.

A second example of this is Yoder's radical claim that every member of the Christian community is gifted.[33] The gist of Yoder's description of "The Fullness of Christ"[34] is that every member is empowered by God. This empowerment does not serve any kind of hierarchical end; instead, it is aimed at correcting such abuses. This little chapter not only makes the radical claim that all members of the community are empowered it also makes the claim that the hierarchical patterns of church leadership stand opposed to this practice. Yoder makes the claim that of all the practices he discusses in this book it is this one that continues to await its reformation.

This last clue is representative of the discord between Yoder and Hauerwas. Hauerwas' vision of the Christian community cannot account for this radical openness to God's empowerment because it founds the order of the community first against the possibility of disorder. Ordering the community takes precedence over the encounter with others and the possibility of internal fracture and growth. Hauerwas most provocative book *Unleashing the Scripture: Freeing the Bible from Captivity to America*[35] demonstrates his unwillingness to allow for such empowerment. The main thrust of this book is to convince American Christians that they are too individualistic to be trusted with the Bible. American Christians do not possess the necessary vision or skills to read the Bible. Therefore, it is better that the Bible is taken out of their hands so that a community governing body can control its appropriation. Such a maneuver still demonstrates the confining nature of the tradition based community. Hauerwas does not recognize that part of what made the reformation possible is how the texts were made available to all the members of the congregation. Certainly such a practice is open

---

the Church," 310. Yoder's description of tradition in these terms is found in his article "The Authority of Tradition" in *Priestly Kingdom*, 69.

32. Ibid., 311.
33. Yoder, *Body Politics*.
34. Ibid., 47–60.
35. Hauerwas, *Unleashing the Scripture*.

to abuse, but to remove the texts from the congregation is to close off the possibility of an internal critique.

Coles' use of the term "patience" is an excellent clue to Yoder's position and it helps to show that for Yoder such concerns about tradition were not as important as they were for Hauerwas. In the article "'Patience' as Method in Moral Reasoning: Is An Ethic of Discipleship 'Absolute?'"[36] Yoder provides an interesting description that coincides with Hauerwas' concern above. He describes a situation in which he is visiting a Sunday School class at his church. Yoder argues that if someone says something contrary to a traditional value it is not his place to fix his/her comment. He argues that it is not a part of his calling to apply his "better wisdom" to instruct the person. Patience surfaces in this example because it indicates "respect for the roles of others."[37] Basically, Yoder's notion of patience strikes against Hauerwas' concern about misuses of the Bible. Certainly Yoder desires that Christian churches follow orthodox patterns of thought and behavior, but he is not as nervous about mistakes like Hauerwas. Yoder was concerned to make sure that at any point God could interrupt the community. Hauerwas' conception of the community does not foster this interruptive potential.

Because of this failure, to read Yoder through the lens of Hauerwas might blind one to the more radical nature of Yoder's work. Hauerwas stands as an important figure because in most ways he does read Yoder well. He answers the modified claim of Gustafson to provide a philosophical framework for helping to translate the claims of Yoder into current discourses, but his use of MacIntyre ends up misconstruing these radical elements of Yoder's thought by attempting to tame "The Wild Patience of John Howard Yoder."[38]

Chris K. Huebner: Exilic Christianity

Of these three Yoder supporters, Huebner's work is closest to the aims of this project. In fact, his reading of Yoder's work stands as one of the significant motivations for linking Yoder with Levinas. Like Hauerwas and Carter, Huebner believes that Yoder' work remains relevant for contemporary

---

36. Yoder, "'Patience' as Method in Moral Reasoning: Is An Ethic of Discipleship 'Absolute?'" in *Wisdom of the Cross*, 24–42.

37. Ibid., 29.

38. Coles, "Wild Patience of John Howard Yoder: 'Outsiders' and the 'Otherness of the Church,'" 305–31.

Christian theological and ethical discourse. Huebner also generates his extension of Yoder through links with aspects of the Western philosophical tradition. Unlike Hauerwas and Carter, however, Huebner employs a radically different set of thinkers to construct his supplementary edifice. The bulk of Huebner's work is contained in his recent collection of essays *A Precarious Peace*.[39] Huebner's essays contain efforts to link Yoder with thinkers like Foucault and Derrida. Huebner's work is different because he operates with thinkers largely associated with the contemporary Continental viewpoints of the philosophical tradition. Although he is not alone in mining this strand of philosophy for ways to extend Yoder,[40] his efforts are part of a new strategy for interpreting Yoder. This approach has reenergized interest for Yoder's work while simultaneously opening numerous trajectories of uncharted possibilities for the interpretation of it. Huebner's approach is not wrongly portrayed when it is pictured as pioneering work.

Huebner's work is best read when it is placed against the work of Carter and Hauerwas. For Carter, the link between Yoder and the classical orthodoxy of the 4th and 5th centuries ran the risk of systematizing Yoder's thought; i.e. subjecting Yoder's work to a Constantinian strategy. Basically, Carter's effort failed to maintain Yoder's ambivalence to that material thereby aligning him too closely with the empire building elements of the creedal and confessional work of early Christianity. Hauerwas, on the other hand, effectively maintained Yoder's stance against Constantinianism in terms of his engagement with outside sources of information. Hauerwas faithfully illuminated Yoder's historicism regarding universal truths and the possibility of developing a stand-alone natural theology. He excluded, however, this historicism from his portrayal of the Christian community. Hauerwas' conception of the Christian tradition in terms of its own self-awareness failed to maintain Yoder's recognition that the fact that one is "always working with a grain of the universe" is as much an issue within the church as it is outside of it. Huebner's work, then, is an effort to push beyond Carter and Hauerwas by attaining a compelling Yoderian response to his critics while simultaneously maintaining the authenticity of Yoder's purposes.

The clarification and dismissal of these mischaracterizations of Yoder's work is one of Huebner's chief aims. His article "Globalization, Theory,

---

39. Huebner, *Precarious Peace*.

40. The book by Ben C. Ollengurger and Gayle Goober Koontz, *A Mind Patient and Untamed*, contains a number of pieces that operate along this same trajectory.

and Dialogical Vulnerability" articulates that "the peace of Christ is negated when it is articulated by a medium that is somehow implicated in the expression of violence."[41] Huebner's reading of Yoder is careful to retain Yoder's sensitivity to the breadth of violence. He realizes that Yoder recognized how violence traveled beyond its physical manifestation. Huebner argues that many of Yoder's supporters fail to take this state of affairs into account when they offer their interpretation of his work. Nancey Murphy's attempt to recast Yoder's pacifism in terms of a Lakatosian research program is a prime example of this problem.[42] Murphy attempts to show that Yoder's construal of pacifism is viable in that it reflects the nature of this research program. This means that, like the Lakatosian program, Yoder's articulation of pacifism must be shown to be false in terms that would force a radical reappraisal of its basic features. In other words, substantial forms of counterevidence must be produced in order to demonstrate the invalid nature of his program. Yoder's pacifism, then, stands and falls on the ability to muster evidence or counterevidence rather than on the person and work of Jesus. According to Huebner, Murphy has not only attempted to turn Yoder's work into a large scale system, but she has also argued for its validation in terms of its effectiveness. For Murphy, the reason that Yoder's pacifism is a valid theological project is because of its results. Huebner points out that this runs counter to Yoder's repudiation of instrumental thinking. Yoder was a pacifist because Jesus was, not because it is a better methodology for making the world come out right. Quoting from Yoder's *Politics*, Huebner is able to show that Jesus' political vision cannot be linked to instrumental thinking: "it involves giving up the Constantinian assumption that it is up to us to guarantee that history comes out right."[43] Cause and effect cannot be the primary element of articulating Yoder's position; such efforts end up aligning Yoder's work with violent strategies. Huebner argues that "dialogical vulnerability" cannot be established through such means.

Huebner's point here is that one's epistemological basis and approach, even a pacifist one, can contain violent strands. Many of Yoder's supporters fail to recognize this element when they attempt to appropriate Yoder's work. Huebner highlights that Yoder was just as concerned with these

41. Huebner, "Globalization, Theory, and Dialogical Vulnerability: John Howard Yoder and the Possibility of a Pacifist Epistemology" in *Precarious Peace*, 97–113 (97).

42. Ibid., 107–9. Murphy's article, "John Howard Yoder's Systematic Defence of Christian Pacifism," is located in *Wisdom of the Cross*, 45–68.

43. Huebner, "Globalization, Theory, and Dialogical Vulnerability: John Howard Yoder and the Possibility of a Pacifist Epistemology" in *Precarious Peace*, 108.

epistemological forms of violence as he was with physical manifestations of it. This necessity to account for both physical and epistemological forms of violence is what leads Huebner to look toward the more radical thinkers within the Western philosophical tradition. He recognizes that thinkers like Derrida or Foucault have already begun examining and discussing both forms of violence. They offer the possibility of rereading Yoder without having to choose between the two forms of violence.

One of the alluring aspects of the work of contemporary Continental thinkers is their penchant for thinking in and through the uncertainties of human existence. Huebner views how this destabilizing element works to open up new lines of thinking. For example, Huebner draws from Foucault's critique of the human subject as a foundation of knowledge. Huebner notes that "Foucault claims that the modern idea of the subject as foundation is but one more attempt to ground truth in a kind of original source and thus to secure or seize truth by means of a violent will to power."[44] Foucault's work is important for its ability to recognize both forms of violence. Huebner finds here that Foucault is interested in exposing the deeper epistemological forms of violence as it seeks to control and secure a base of power. For Huebner this contains many parallels to Yoder's own views of the issues.

A second feature from this assessment is the realization that the human self is an uncertain and ambiguous feature of existence. For Foucault, the self is an unfinished business. Not only does their work signal the incomplete nature of the self, it is also set toward deconstructing those works that would seek to assert a more robust version of the self. The articulation of a destabilized self becomes a counter message to those lines of thought which try to establish a more concrete static description. Huebner believes that this understanding of the self falls more into line with Yoder's own conception. The uncertainty of existence is something that Yoder's work is concerned to maintain and these thinkers offer a way of rearticulating Yoder's material without compromising this commitment to uncertainty. Huebner's work, then, is basically an effort to show that Yoder is also interested in deconstructing efforts to seize power.[45] Uniting Yoder with these

---

44. Huebner, "The Agony of Truth: Martyrdom, Violence, and Christian Ways of Knowing" in *Precarious Peace*, 140. Huebner primarily utilizes two of Foucault's articles "Truth and Juridical Forms" in *Power, Essential Works of Foucault 1954-1984*, vol. 3, and "About the Beginning of the Hermeneutics of the Self" in *Religion and Culture*.

45. Blum's article "Yoder's Patience and/with Derrida's *Difference*" in *Mind Patient and Untamed*, 75–88 also employs the idea that Yoder's "patience" serves as a way of

Yoder's Rejoinders

thinkers, according to Huebner, results in highlighting this deeper critique of violence within Yoder's thought.

A second move for Huebner is to recognize Yoder's portrayal of the Christian tradition as a community on the move. Like the emphasis on the destabilizing nature of identity, Yoder's construal of the Christian tradition in terms of movement helps to eliminate the effort to seize power that is brought on by institutionalization and stability. Huebner's analysis of Paul Virilio's conception of war as speed helps to illuminate this point.[46] Virilio's work is aimed at highlighting the underlying elements of warfare. His work is an effort to illuminate the assumptions and axioms through which the act of war is based. One contribution is his construal of war as a race to secure the ever moving landscape—it is a "dromology."[47] This conception of war as a race is derivative from his larger claim that one of the chief factors in political discourse is speed. He argues that "wealth is an aspect of speed. One usually says that power is tied in with wealth. In my opinion, it's tied in first and foremost with speed; wealth comes afterward."[48] The insight here is that most people believe that wealth drives war, but Virilio argues that this works to blind us from the deeper nature of warfare. War is, for Virilio, a race to secure and control the movement of existence. Speed is the deeper aspect of warfare because war is a race to harness the forces of existence. Huebner elaborates Virilio's findings by illuminating his three stages of the conduct of warfare. First, war is fought with instruments of obstruction. Second, war is fought with weapons of destruction. Third, the contemporary stage, war is "the deployment of weapons of communication."[49] Huebner describes the crux of Virilio's comments when he comments that "(t)he logic of violence unfolds and intensifies, war is becoming less and less about territory and more about the management of information."[50] The point is that war has shifted away from domination of landscapes to a domination

---

deconstructing theological certainties.

46. The bulk of Huebner's comments are recorded in his article "Patience, Witness, and the Scattered Body of Christ: Yoder and Virilio on Knowledge, Politics and Speed" in *Precarious Peace*, 115–32. The major source text for Virilio's work that Huebner analyzes is his *Speed and Politics*.

47. I borrow this from Benjamin H. Bratton's insightful introduction, "Logistics of Habitable Circulation," in *Speed and Politics*, 7–25 (8).

48. Virilio and Lotringer, *Pure War*, 57.

49. Huebner, "Patience, Witness, and the Scattered Body of Christ: Yoder and Virilio on Knowledge, Politics and Speed" in *Precarious Peace*, 119.

50. Ibid., 119–20.

of knowledge—information is the new frontier. Speed is essential, then, because the first to harness and direct the flow of information will reap the rewards of military success.

The end result of this emphasis on speed is the dissolution of conversation. Dialogue is removed from politics because it takes too long to work through. Virilio borrows an example from the World Cup soccer games to demonstrate the shift from conversation and event to production.[51] Virilio argues that an inversion takes place with the advent of radio and television. The ability to broadcast the game beyond the boundaries of the stadium makes the participants of that event "superfluous." The shift of power moves from participant to outside viewer; one no longer has to be there in order to be an expert on the situation. I can judge, from my comfortable recliner, the events and situations around the world without ever having to be there. Politics as conversation disappears because all of the conversation is contained in the broadcast; rather than working through issues and concerns, politics is now about metanarratives—it is consumed by the viewer. The main thrust of this is that warfare is undertaken through the control and dissemination of information. The faster that one is able to render an account of things, the faster that one is able to mobilize the masses against the enemy. Negotiation is no longer necessary.

Huebner makes a correlation between Virilio's argument that speed eliminates political conversation and Yoder's stress on methodological patience. This idea of patience is an outgrowth of Yoder's commitment to pacifism; "it assumes that truthfulness is an utterly contingent gift that can only be given and received and that it emerges at the site of vulnerable interchange with the other."[52] The correlation is supported by Huebner's argument that Yoder's "patience" is not only a recognition of the latent violence within metanarrative formulations but also in the way that knowledge is transferred. The speed of delivery, which interconnects with Virilio's material, is also a violent feature because it closes off conversations. The overarching point is that this rush to control or disperse information is prevalent in the activity of "developing sweeping historical narratives that are not subject to ongoing self-critical scrutiny;"[53] the articulation of a particular historical epoch closes off any further discussion of how that par-

---

51. Virilio and Lotringer, *Pure War*, 99–100.

52. Huebner, "Patience, Witness, and the Scattered Body of Christ: Yoder and Virilio on Knowledge, Politics and Speed" in *Precarious Peace*, 126.

53. Ibid., 127.

ticular epoch is to be understood. The act of dialoguing about that material is arrested because there is no need to talk. A speedy delivery eliminates the need to take the long road of patient conversations. Yoder's commitment to pacifism is a commitment to such dialogue; patience is a form of politics where vulnerable giving and sharing are practiced without attempts to wrest control from the other.

At first glance all of the above appears to make interesting inroads into the nature of knowledge and its interrelationship with violence. Critics, however, have pointed out that Virilio's implicit turn to the slow character of political dialogue does not actually eradicate the problem. This discussion of the importance of politics "remains committed to a concentric model of identity as a closed and bounded site of power."[54] In other words, returning to the slow work of political dialogue is still very much open to being manipulated by the first two stages of war: obstruction and destruction. The immediate concern is that Yoder's work stands in connection with this critique of Virilio; i.e. pacifism is just as capable of employing its own variations of obstruction and destruction (as well as speed). It is not enough to maintain that political conversation is necessary; such conversations can still be harnessed through efforts of production.[55] The point is that even with Yoder's insistence that patience mark one's conversational approach, it is still open to oppressive efforts.

Huebner points to Yoder's construal of the Christian tradition as a community on the move as a way to avoid this danger. This recognition that the community is on the move helps to stave off the temptation to establish and maintain clear spaces of power and control. In contrast to the ways of obstruction and destruction, Yoder's portrayal of the Christian community is based in movement rather than settlement. The attempt to mark off and capture space is eliminated because there is no final absolute space from which Christians could stand. Huebner articulates that Christians should posture themselves to a "receptivity to God's ongoing generosity" rather than toward attempts of "preservation."[56] The "scattered body of Christ" serves as a stop gap against those attempts, even within pacifist circles, to control and secure a space of power. Exile rather than preservation is

---

54. Ibid., 123.

55. Interestingly, Virilio notes this very phenomenon in his description of the politics of Ancient Greece. Virilio and Lotringer, *Pure War*, 99–100.

56. Huebner, "Patience, Witness, and the Scattered Body of Christ: Yoder and Virilio on Knowledge, Politics and Speed" in *Precarious Peace*, 125.

The Trace of the Face in the Politics of Jesus

the catchword for the Christian community. Completion is endlessly deferred; the community is called daily to work out its salvation with fear and trembling.

Huebner's work clearly has implications for responding to Reimer and Gustafson. The deepening of Yoder through Virilio offers important contributions to discussions of epistemological concerns. Yet, Huebner's work is also effective for illuminating some of the deeper elements of Yoder's descriptions of Christian practice, especially revolutionary subordination. Schüssler Fiorenza argued that the concept of revolutionary subordination undercut the impetus to seek change. Yoder's invitation for Christians to subordinate themselves to their socio-political contexts, even if they are oppressive, appears to reverse the great amount of progress that people have achieved for making the world less oppressive. Huebner's analysis provides important insights for formulating an answer to this concern. The first point it raises is Yoder's assertion that justice is a relative concept.[57] Yoder's point is not that justice changes with each and every day, but rather that no one is able to surmount the particularities of everyday existence in order to view the totality of justice. The development of just structures is a continual, if not permanent, process. This connects well with Huebner's linking of Yoder to Foucault's destabilization of the human self. Yoder understood well that a lack of certainty underlay any effort to comprehensively conceptualize human experience. Huebner's description of the Christian tradition as a diasporic community helps to keep that tradition from falsely seeking totality and completion. The recognition of a continual movement underscores the ambiguous nature of existence. This characterization places all claims for justice into question. The point is not to eliminate efforts to seek justice, but rather to heighten the need for a cautionary approach to that task.

More importantly, however, is Huebner's ability to illuminate Yoder's response to Schüssler Fiorenza regarding the belief that he and she want the same thing.[58] Yoder reiterates that he views revolutionary subordination as a way of engaging the wider context rather than a way of managing church life. He does not disagree with Schüssler Fiorenza that these texts were used (misused from his position) to enforce a male hegemony within the Christian tradition, but he thinks that this is a misreading. Yoder argued that the original trajectory of these codes was hijacked and silenced by persons

---

57. Yoder, "Christian and Capital Punishment," 1–23.
58. Yoder, *Politics of Jesus*, 188–92.

wanting to institute that hegemonic program. This concluding comment helps to distinguish the difference Yoder seeks to portray.

> Elisabeth Schüssler Fiorenza cited this sentence but reversed its meaning into "it motivates Christian slaves and women to accept 'things as they are.'" In that passage the formulation of "things as they are" was that in Christ (and in baptism) the differences between "Jew and Greek, slave and free, male and female" have been transcended. That is in some important sense "real." Yet Jews are still Jewish and Greeks Greek; that also is "real." Both reality claims and social strategies need to be more nuanced. What the Haustafeln texts project is a tactic for change in the light of the new Christological reality.[59]

Yoder believes that Schüssler Fiorenza fails to understand his use of the phrase "accepting things as they are." What he points out is that early Christians found themselves with a foot in two worlds: on the one hand, Christians were now part of a unity that transcended all of their previous distinctions—they were one in Christ; on the other hand, these distinctions continued to exist—they were still Jews and Gentiles. Yoder's notion of revolutionary subordination, then, was a tactic. It was meant to help these Christians to faithfully navigate this divide. What Yoder implies, but does not directly state, is that revolutionary subordination is a practice that handles this reality without having to resort to violence. Huebner's work helps to confirm this. Revolutionary subordination was a means to enact the freedom and unity these Christians felt without having to force it on those who stood outside of the community. Yoder was critical of theologies of liberation not for their attempt to discern and articulate injustices, but rather because of their inability to fully divorce themselves from the assumptions of their oppressors. In other words, it is not just that liberators often use violence to bring about change (although he was critical of this too), but that the change they hope to bring is not fully divested of the assumptions and axioms of their oppressor. The liberating movements only end up exchanging one tyrant for another. They fail to attend to their own underlying violent assumptions. Revolutionary subordination is a practice aimed at illuminating this unseen commitment to violence. It is aware of the fact that violence runs deeper than its physical manifestation. The ability to subordinate oneself to the current relational structures wards off these deeper alliances with violence because it maintains the perception that

---

59. Ibid., 192.

The Trace of the Face in the Politics of Jesus

Christianity is a community on the move. The exilic nature of this community aids the development and maintenance of dialogue and vulnerability. In each case, a patient methodology replaces an all too hasty effort to fix a situation through other means. Dialogue and vulnerability mark Yoder's notion of the Christian community and revolutionary subordination is a practice built to manifest and maintain these marks.

The portrayal of Christianity in exile rather than at home is both the strength and weakness of Huebner's work. The exilic picture is a strong point because it enables Huebner to be true to Yoder in ways that Carter and Hauerwas fail to accomplish. The picture of Christianity on the move stifles efforts to codify him into a set of propositions. Thinkers like Virilio and Foucault draw attention to this exilic element within Yoder's work. These thinkers embody the prophetic nature Yoder associates with the exilic community of Christianity. Huebner faithfully characterizes Yoder's unwillingness to finally commit himself to any one position. He recognizes the fluidity of Yoder's work and resists trying to place a foreign system of coherence onto that work in order to complete its trajectory.

The weakness of Huebner's approach is the lack of a delineation of the originary nature of violence; he fails to ask into the origins of violence. Huebner claims that certain modes of existence carry latent violent tendencies, yet he does not plumb the depths of violence. The work of Virilio and Foucault help him to identify these latent forms of violence through their discussions of the speed of delivery or systems of control, but this only highlights its underlying existence. Huebner may be concerned about marking these contours of violence because it would run the risk of turning his work into an absolute position. The fact that violence plays such a central role for his work, however, demands a more complete discussion of those marks. The effort to delineate the initial forms of violence does not have to be characterized in absolute terms. Naming more clearly the movement of violence, especially in its latent phases, helps to initiate the process of filtering it out. Yoder's Constantinianism is one effort to name the contours of violence that does not exhaustively describe it. The refusal to push deeper into the inner workings of violence leaves him open to falling prey to it.

Conclusion: Setting the Stage for Levinas

These three brief sketches of contemporary Yoder supporters demonstrate that Yoder's work possess elements to answer the charges leveled by his critics. Although these answers counter the critiques against Yoder's work they do it at the price of losing something of Yoder's thought. For Carter, the attempt to portray Yoder in terms of the Christian theological work of the 4th and 5th century countered Reimer's suggestion that Yoder totally rejected the works of that period. Carter rightly pointed out that Yoder appreciated parts of that material. Nevertheless, Carter's connection of Yoder to that tradition failed to account for some of the suspicions Yoder continued to hold. The main threat was the effort of those thinkers to create an ahistorical comprehensive account of Christian convictions. The formulations that developed out of that tradition sought to combat arising heresies and to articulate permanent and universal features of the Christian tradition. Carter's attachment of Yoder to the first aspect is accurate, but he does not account for the latter feature. Carter's assessment that Yoder appreciated that part of the Christian tradition did not fully address Yoder's suspicions of the desire for articulating the permanent features of Christianity. Carter's account needs more nuance to answer Reimer's charge. Making the distinction between the practical trajectory of classical orthodoxy (to ward off heresies) and the metaphysical trajectory (to locate the universal truths of Christian claims) could go a long way to disarming Reimer's challenge while simultaneously maintaining Yoder's reticence toward comprehensive metaphysical accounts of Christianity. Metaphysical speculation is something that Yoder's work rejects and Carter's account fails to maintain this rejection.

Hauerwas' efforts are much closer to Yoder's intentions, especially with regard to the engagement between Christianity and its wider context. Hauerwas maintains the importance of not trying to make Christianity into a set of universally accessible philosophical categories that could be justified outside of the Christian experience. Alongside of this is Hauerwas' effort to link Yoder's thought with a philosophical base to help extend its content. Hauerwas believed that an implicit criticism of "enlightenment" moral strategies existed within Yoder's work. Hauerwas posited that MacIntyre's thoroughgoing critique of those projects helped to tease this implicit argument out of Yoder's work. This attachment of Yoder and MacIntyre provided a more developed answer to Gustafson's dichotomy between authenticity and intelligibility. Hauerwas' combination described more clearly the inability for locating a universal medium for making sensible claims while simultaneously showing how such efforts actually undermine important feature of a tradition's moral capacities. The downside of this combination, however, was the way that Hauerwas' conception of the Christian church, which is very much informed by MacIntyre, diverged from Yoder's conception. One particular divergence lies in Hauerwas' description of the internal operations of the Christian community. Hauerwas' use of MacIntyre fails to appreciate the radical nature of Yoder's articulation of the "free church tradition." The stress on tradition, especially its security from outside influences, ends up muting Yoder's portrayal of the Christian community as radically vulnerable and receptive. Yoder's notion that every member of the community is gifted for service is stifled by the necessity of erecting structures of control. The need to maintain the tradition in the face of opponents, both without and within, overrides this radical conception; vulnerability is minimized to help maintain the security of the community.

Chris Huebner's work offers the most authentic explication of Yoder's work. Huebner does not hesitate to link Yoder with philosophical sources, but he makes sure that these conversation partners are made to illuminate Yoder's thought not to overtake it. Huebner's attempt to demonstrate the constructive components of Yoder's work maintains its radical nature. The heart of Huebner's work is maintaining Yoder's commitment to peace and nonviolence. Huebner believes that the efforts of most of his supporters are still embedded in a kind of latent violence, which is intellectual as well as physical. The innovative aspect of Yoder's thought is his recognition of the depths to which violence can sink. Huebner believes that what many of Yoder's supporters miss is this ever present commitment to recognizing and avoiding violent strategies. Huebner's work is an attempt to bring this recognition out and to try and maintain its central importance. Huebner recognizes the depths of violence, but doesn't fully express the origins of that violence. Huebner recognizes that violence is embedded in human existence, but he does not fundamentally unpack the link between this existence and its attachment to latent violence. The authors that Huebner utilizes to help tease out Yoder's deeper critiques of violence must always also be argued against. In other words, Huebner allows these authors to point to this deeper analysis of violence, but he resists making constructive efforts toward Yoder through these thinkers. They are merely luminaries for Yoder's work. They are not useful for helping to answer key questions regarding Yoder's analysis of violence. Questions like: what did Yoder think that was the cause of violence or what does it mean that we want to grasp the controls of history?

This reading of Carter, Hauerwas, and Huebner invites further reflection and exploration. Huebner's work is particularly helpful because unlike most Yoder supporters he is willing to connect Yoder's work with that of more radical thinkers. This utilization of the "genealogical"[60] tradition carves out a new niche for Yoderian explorations. The link of Yoder to a thinker like Levinas is no longer unthinkable. The next chapter seeks to pursue what a link to Levinas could look like. This chapter, however, can only be made possible by examining the processes of those Yoder supporters who have extended him through the work of a philosophical thinker. Although this chapter locates negative aspects with each thinker's effort to restate Yoder, they continue to serve as a validation for seeking to tease out deeper aspects of Yoder's work in philosophical terms.

---

60. I am borrowing this term from MacIntyre's account. MacIntyre, *Three Rival Versions of Moral Enquiry*.

chapter four

The Kenotic Bridge

An Experimental Response through a Levinasian Rereading of Yoder's Methodology and Revolutionary Subordination

Introduction

THUS FAR, THE PROJECT has made the argument that the insights of Yoder's work remain relevant for Christian moral and theological reflection. This relevance, though, is aided by linking Yoder with the work of another thinker, especially someone from within the Western philosophical tradition. The question that remains, however, is which author is best suited for achieving this end. To whom should we turn that will enable us to extend his work while retaining his voice? The danger of misconstruing Yoder's work is very easy to accomplish. Our previous chapter highlighted how some of Yoder's best interpreters can produce this error. Nonetheless, even with these failings these interpreters verify the necessity of extending his work beyond its initial scope. Their work stands as an invitation to continue to locate a framework that will illuminate and extend Yoder's insights without losing his voice.

Emmanuel Levinas is an excellent choice for two reasons. First, the attempt to link Yoder with Levinas has yet to be taken up. Levinas' work remains an untapped resource for illuminating aspects of Yoder's thought.

The Kenotic Bridge

Peter Blum's essay "Yoder's Patience and/ with Derrida's *Differance*,"[1] as well as Huebner's work are two of the closest parallels with my attempt to link Yoder with a thinker from the Continental aspect of the philosophical tradition.[2] The fact that Yoder spent a good portion of his life in Europe might imply a possible relationship to some of the concerns and problems that mark that philosophical tradition. Certainly, Yoder's wariness of philosophy would hinder a full blown acceptance, but the close geographical relationship between this philosophical tradition and his theological training might indicate some interesting parallels. Second, portions of Levinas' work echo those of Yoder. For instance, one aspect of Levinas' work is dedicated to extracting the particular from the universal or reinscribing the significance of concrete particularities of human existence over against the desire for universal essences of that same experience. This clearly contains parallels to Yoder's suspicions regarding methodological work. Yoder's worries about the search for a universal methodology also contain a concern for the loss of the particularity of Christian experience. The fact of these parallels creates the possibility for generating a link between Levinas and Yoder without having to reduce each thinker to the other.

This chapter proceeds by examining two aspects of Levinas' work: the critique of ontology and the phenomenological description of the encounter of the face of the other. The main thesis of this chapter is that these two conceptions clarify and extend Yoder's methodological approach and articulation of revolutionary subordination. The net result is that one can describe Yoder's work in terms of a philosophy of otherness; i.e. that the politics of Jesus are a politics of otherness. The chapter begins by addressing Chris Huebner's resistance against attaching Levinas to Yoder's work. Basing his position on the work of Gillian Rose, Huebner argues that attaching Levinas to Yoder reinscribes the criticisms that Yoder is "sectarian." The problem with Huebner's analysis, however, is that Rose's interpretation of Levinas is not the final word. Huebner's reliance on Rose closes off other readings of Levinas, not to mention that it asserts that Levinas is also, by default, a sectarian thinker. A counter interpretation can and will be provided that demonstrates the legitimacy of Levinas' work for establishing a link to Yoder.

---

1. Blum, "Yoder's Patience and/ with Derrida's *Difference*" in *Mind Patient and Untamed*, 75–88.
2. Yoder's relationship to Karl Barth, of course, has been widely attested.

The chapter will then move to describe the contours of these two Levinasian concepts. A description is given with regard to their definition and use within Levinas' work. After providing these descriptions the chapter will move to illuminate the bridge for establishing the link between Levinas and Yoder. The idea that will be used is the notion of kenosis. The concept of kenosis opens the door to reread Yoder's methodological approach and articulation of revolutionary subordination as components of a philosophy of otherness. This experimental linkage will demonstrate that one can speak of Yoder's work as fundamentally committed to otherness while simultaneously retaining Yoder's claim that Jesus is the center of all Christian moral and theological discourse. Translating Yoder's work into a philosophy of otherness does not lose sight of the fact that, for Yoder, Jesus is the embodiment and example of this philosophy.

Why Not Levinas?: A Reappraisal of Huebner's Rejection of Levinas

The importance of Chris Huebner's work cannot be understated. His work, which has been noted above, stands in close proximity to my own. In fact, Huebner also desires to recast Yoder's work in terms of otherness. The difference between Huebner and this project, however, is the evaluation of Levinas as a suitable conversational partner. Huebner argues that Levinas is problematic because he moves Yoder back toward the sectarian reading of his work. I believe that this is a mistaken view of Levinas' contribution. The link between Yoder and Levinas is profitable for combatting those criticisms.

Huebner's rejection of Levinas is based on the idea that he still "participates in a violent vision of truth as ownership."[3] According to Huebner, Levinas forgoes the destabilizing concept of the human person by asserting that the self is founded on the relationship to the other. This fails to link with Yoder's claim "that Christ is the truth."[4] This claim is "counter-epistemology" because it fails to deliver certainty. It is "an essentially agonizing and agonistic reality."[5] The problem with Levinas, then, is that his work points to a settled position. Drawing from the work of Gillian Rose,

---

3. Huebner, "The Agony of Truth: Martyrdom, Violence, and Christian Ways of Knowing" in *Precarious Peace*, 141.

4. Ibid., 133.

5. Ibid., 134.

Huebner criticizes Levinas' attention and priority of the other as postulating a "one-way sacrificial orientation."[6] In other words, Levinas' position can be reduced to the proposition that each person is infinitely responsible for the other person; self-sacrifice is the absolute mode of human existence. This "truth," once realized, leads to a decision to abnegate oneself in service to others. The problem is that the self, who is called to sacrifice, remains unscathed by that call. He/She retains full mastery over him/herself. "(T)he logic of self-sacrifice continues to presume the power of the self to give itself up."[7] Certainty resurfaces in the move to make oneself into a sacrifice; a universal essence opens up and the nature of the self is secured. For Huebner, this claim of certainty carries within it an inherent form of violence. The establishment of this truth secures a base of power and authority from which a comprehensive knowledge can be detailed and implemented.

Mastery of truth and the violence embedded in such mastery are only one part of Huebner's concerns with Levinas. Drawing again from Rose's analysis, he highlights that Levinas' work is also guilty of proposing a utopian solution. It is utopian because it posits peace outside of the fray of experience or existence. This idea of a self, which self-sacrifices for the other, is an absolute peace. This truth exists outside of the push and pull of everyday experience thereby making it too idealistic and impractical for real life. Basically, all of the answers to life's questions are summarized in the reality that one is responsible for the other. This is directly reminiscent of criticisms leveled against absolute pacifists who are thought to believe that if everyone would lay down their weapons all conflicts would cease. The reality, however, is that conflict continues to exist. Rose describes it in this way: "this is experience—the struggle to know, and still to misknow, and yet to grow."[8] The idea that self-sacrifice is the final answer fails to account for the nature of reality. Like the absolute pacifists, this conception fails to take seriously the "struggle," error, and "growth" of human experience. Utopian solutions posit that the conflict of actual existence is easily overcome by self-abnegation. The mere sacrifice of one's own concerns is not likely to usher in a time of peaceful bliss.

Huebner's rejection of Levinas, then, is based on these two ideas. Levinas' work contains a call for self-sacrifice and this reinscribes a robust

6. Ibid., 141.
7. Ibid., 141.
8. Rose, *Broken Middle: Out of Our Ancient Society*, 263–64 quoted in Huebner, "The Agony of Truth: Martyrdom, Violence, and Christian Ways of Knowing" in *Precarious Peace*, 142.

subjectivity, which contains the "ownership of truth" mentality and the positing of a simple "other-worldly" solution. Linking Yoder to Levinas, then, will only reinforce the criticisms leveled at Yoder's work. Yoder's call for Christians to be nonviolent is viewed as failing to recognize the necessity for coercion (a la Niebuhr) in a world of competing self-interested people. This means that his call for nonviolence is a call to withdraw from social issues and concerns. The attempt to frame Yoder's work in Levinasian terms can only solidify the penchant of Yoderian critics to slough off his insights by strengthening their observation that Yoder's work, although novel and interesting, is really not helpful for developing Christian theological and moral discourse.

Huebner's rejection of Levinas, however, is based on a contested reading of his work. One of the glaring weaknesses of Huebner's claims against Levinas is that he fails to trace out Rose's critique through the Levinas corpus. This is not to say that Rose's work on Levinas is blatantly false, but a closer examination of Levinas' work would be instrumental for deciding whether Rose's critique fully captures the aims of Levinas. It is quite possible that Gillian Rose's reading of Levinas is not the final word. Numerous readers of Levinas' work have come to very different conclusions. One particular Levinas scholar, Martin Kavka, has directly countered the criticisms that Rose puts forward. Kavka provides an evaluative examination of Rose's critique as well as a demonstration that Levinas can be read in another way.[9]

Kavka provides a description which delineates the parameters of Rose's critique.[10] According to Kavka, Rose argues that Levinas' work conceives a separation between "the violence of ontology in the order of being" and "the realm beyond being."[11] This means that Levinas argues for a two-tiered universe where the logistics of everyday existence are separated from the transcendent "realm beyond being." The import of this separation is that the transcendent realm cannot be known by the participants of existence; an unbridgeable void exists between them. The fact of this inability to know translates into an inability to develop "moral imperatives."[12] The transcendent realm, the realm which holds the answers to life's questions, is incapable of being accessed due to the separation. The need for moral norms cannot be assuaged by looking to this transcendent realm—it

9. Kavka, "Saying Kadish for Gillian Rose, or on Levinas and *Geltungsphilosophie*" in *Secular Theology*, 104–29.

10. Ibid., 109.

11. Ibid.

12. Ibid.

"has no relation to the real world in which we live and breathe."[13] This inability to locate moral norms undercuts the desire to perform ethically; "if consciousness does not have the power to formulate moral imperatives, it certainly cannot have the power to act morally."[14]

Kavka's description reveals that the second of Huebner's two critiques is the frame for both. Huebner's worry about a robust identity goes hand in hand with his concerns about the "utopian" basis of Levinas' work. Rose's critique of Levinas is that he conceives a solution which is founded in an untranslatable void between actual existence and the perfect solution. The desire to find moral norms in this unreachable beyond creates a blind spot to the unsettled nature of real existence. Because one's attention is directed to bridging the unbridgeable one is less likely to understand the complexity of real human existence. In effect, one is always turning away from the real problems of existence toward a speculative transcendent realm. This speculative turn helps to create easy solutions that only compound the problems. For instance, the claim that one is to abnegate oneself for the other is an all too easy solution. Not only does it fail to recognize the complexity of inter-subjective experience it also fails because it reinscribes a robust identity or consciousness which can lead to a mode of tyranny. Self-sacrifice erases the ambiguity of human existence by giving it an absolute pathway. It overcomes "the struggle to recognize: to know, and still to misknow, and yet to grow."

Huebner claims that Levinas' work does not provide an unsettled identity and that he does not offer a solution that accounts for the reality of conflict. Kavka argues, however, that Rose's critique, which is the basis for Huebner's rejection, does not quite fully appreciate the logic of Levinas' work. Levinas, when read more thoroughly, provides an account of the unsettled identity and a conception of reality that recognizes the agony of conflict in its movement toward peace. Kavka details how Levinas' work achieves these important aspects by reexamining Levinas' critical appropriation of the work of Edmund Husserl.

According to Kavka, Levinas recognizes in Husserl's work undeveloped avenues or ambiguous passages which recognize and contest the dominance of the ego running prevalently through his work.[15] Drawing from Husserl's paragraph 56 in *Ideas II*, Kavka is able to demonstrate Levinas' recognition that "here, it is not phenomena that depend upon conscious-

13. Ibid.
14. Ibid.
15. Ibid., 116–20.

ness, but consciousness that depends upon the phenomenon."[16] Husserl's description of inter-subjective human experience recognizes the give and take of that relationship. Consciousness discovers its limits because it must wait on the other to present him/herself to me. Consciousness, then, does not constitute the phenomena; it waits for the phenomena to give itself. This period of waiting creates the space necessary for inverting the direction of intentionality—it is a challenge to the constituting intentionality of one's ego. For Levinas, this inversion works against the dominance of the ego because it remembers that the very possibility of thinking of the other is predicated on his/her approach. Levinas extends the ambiguity of Husserl's recognition of the interaction between consciousness and phenomena into a proof of the transcendental priority of the other over the ego. This priority is an interruption of the ego; it is an unsettling of one's identity. Kavka is quick to note, however, that this interruption is not a complete destruction of the ego; it is, instead, both the possibility for the ego to conceptualize the other person in that the other gives itself to be thought, but simultaneously it checks this power to "thematize"[17] by resisting one's efforts to exhaustively know the other.

> Existence in Levinas is *always* agonistic: the subject asserts itself, the meaning of this assertion is contested by another perspective or by the object's transcendental priority, and then the subject asserts itself anew, and differently, in the light of this new assertion. It is obvious that there is never any complete epistemological security in Levinas' elucidation of the nature of phenomenological subjectivity.[18]

Kavka's illuminative comment here encapsulates the thrust of Levinas' thinking. The distance between the phenomena that gives itself and the constituting consciousness creates an "agonistic" context where give and take, contrary to Rose and Huebner, mark Levinasian identity. Contrary to the idea that Levinas' call for a robust subject to completely abnegate him/herself, the presence of the other enforces an ethical dimension which both grounds and restricts the move of the ego. As Kavka notes, the subject continues to assert him/herself, but always with care and consideration because it must wait on the other.

16. Ibid., 120.

17. I am borrowing this term from Levinas' article "God and Philosophy" in *Emmanuel Levinas*, 129–48.

18. Ibid., 121.

All of the above is mostly directed toward the argument that Levinas' notion of subjectivity is robust and violent while also maintaining a commitment to a "utopian" or unrealistic aim as the basis of his ethics. Kavka's work shows that this is a faulty reading of Levinas. Kavka draws from a wider range of Levinas' materials than does either Rose or Huebner. This broader scope enables Kavka to demonstrate the deeper phenomenological elements to Levinas' thought. This attachment to phenomenology helps to bolster the case that Levinas is not seeking to abandon existence by transcending it; instead, it is in and through existence that Levinas makes his case. Levinas does not attempt to ground ethics in certainty, nor does he attempt to posit the origin of ethics is some abstract conception. Kavka's explication of Levinas' agonistic understanding of reality is contained in his reading of an erotic encounter.[19] The nature of this encounter is not otherworldly; it is an event that takes place within space and time. Yet, the encounter contains the portal or window whereby one is able to glimpse the transcendental priority of the other. The ego is both powerful and powerless in this event—asserting and waiting. The fact that this event is a natural occurrence staves off the criticism that Levinas seeks to ground his ethical discourse in a utopian scheme. Transcendence and ethics are not discovered in some abstract conception; instead, they are located in real human experience. Kavka's work demonstrates that Huebner's rejection of Levinas is too hasty. Kavka's work stands as the invitation, then, to begin to explore an imagined relationship between Yoder and Levinas. Contrary to Huebner's claim that Levinas cannot illuminate Yoder's work because of the misgivings of a robust subjectivity and a utopian solution, Kavka establishes that Levinas does foster an agonistic context. This reopens the door for viewing Yoder in terms of Levinas' work.

Levinas' Criticism of Ontology and Description of the Face of the Other

The Critique of Ontology

The opening comments of Levinas' essay "God and Philosophy" help to describe both the operation of ontological thinking and its primacy in the Western philosophical tradition.

---

19. Ibid., 121–22.

The Trace of the Face in the Politics of Jesus

> The philosophical discourse of the West claims the amplitude of an all-encompassing structure or of an ultimate comprehension. It compels every other discourse to justify itself before philosophy.[20]

Ontology is an endeavor that seeks to provide "an all-encompassing structure." This means that ontological reasoning works to define and articulate the contours of existence. This desire for comprehension is the mark of the Western philosophical tradition. Levinas claims that this tradition "compels every other discourse to justify itself." Any claim to knowledge or truth must inhere within the structures articulated by ontology. Ontology, then, works like a metanarrative. If a discourse wants to be taken seriously it must correspond to the "all-encompassing structure" of philosophical thinking. The primacy of ontological thinking is constituted by this desire to attain full comprehension. The goal it sets for itself propels it to its lofty position. The effort to locate and describe a universal language distinguishes this effort from all others. Other discourses are considered inferior because they only work from very particular and limited aims. These are viewed as a portion of the whole therefore they must conform themselves to that larger picture.

The desire of philosophy to account for existence places thinking and knowledge as the primary modes of being. The Western philosophical tradition has sought to unify thought and action. Throughout its history numerous thinkers have put forth systems of thought which were believed to achieve this unification. Levinas argues that over time ontological thinking has come to realize that this unification is not discovered by the elimination of the one for the other. The crowning moment is that both subjective and objective modes can be accessed through actual human experience. The ideal world is discovered as one examines the world of reality. The power and prestige of this philosophical endeavor is its recognition that "all knowledge of relations by which beings are connected or opposed to one another already involve(s) the comprehension of the fact that these relations and these beings exist."[21] The pesky problem of trying to unite subjective and objective modes of knowing is overcome by examining existence. The truth is not "out there" waiting to be found; instead, it is already placed within the dynamic of experience. The give and take nature of existence the portal through which one is able to comprehend existence.

---

20. Levinas, "God and Philosophy" in *Emmanuel Levinas*, 129.
21. Levinas, "Is Ontology Fundamental?" in *Emmanuel Levinas*, 2.

For Levinas, no one has done more to complete the march of the Western philosophical tradition than Martin Heidegger. Heidegger is the tradition's paramount figure because he accomplishes the unification of philosophy's dual purpose: "The abstract question of the meaning of being qua being and the question of the present hour."[22] Heidegger, according to Levinas, was able to bring together philosophy's penchant for abstraction and the importance of everyday human existence. Drawing from Edmund Husserl's conception of phenomenology, Heidegger posited that in order to discover the Being of beings one need only look at human existence. The "ontic" aspect of human existence is the window through which one is able to locate Being in its generality. Being "gives" or manifests itself through the everyday of human life. Heidegger's achievement is founded in his ability to maintain the dual elements of abstraction and actual human existence without having to jettison either one for the other. "The dignity of being the ultimate and royal discourse belongs to Western philosophy because of the strict coinciding of thought, in which philosophy resides, and the idea of reality in which thought thinks."[23] The battle waged between the subjective and objective starting points of philosophical inquiry is won. The victory is achieved not by the conquest of one over the other, but rather by the process whereby each are united to help form the "all-encompassing" comprehension of existence.

The opening stages of Levinas' criticisms of this tradition are articulated in the early pages of his *Totality and Infinity*.[24] He states that "Western philosophy has most often been an ontology: a reduction of the other to the same by interposition of a middle or neutral term that ensures the comprehension of being."[25] Three elements make up this movement: the same, the other, and the neutral term. The comprehension achieved by ontological thinking is brought about by resolving the difference between the same and the other through a neutral middle term. This encounter is calculated and explained by giving it a name (marriage, family, war, etc.). The third term provides knowledge by naming the encounter. In a nutshell, Levinas' critique of ontology is directed at this capacity to reduce the encounter to that term or name—to resolve the encounter into a neutral term.

---

22. Ibid., 3.
23. Levinas, "God and Philosophy" in *Emmanuel Levinas*, 130.
24. Levinas, *Totality and Infinity*.
25. Ibid., 43.

The Trace of the Face in the Politics of Jesus

Deepening this critique, Levinas articulates that ontology fails to adequately account for the encounter between what he calls "the same" and "the other." The same is a philosophical term designating the "journey" of the ego through the world.[26] Levinas describes it as the modality of identification that the I undergoes as it traverses through the world. Although it travels through many changes it retains its sameness through the unity of its journey. The process is what remains fixed in the ego. The other, however, interrupts this journey by placing it into question. The other resists being assimilated into this process of identification. Ontology seeks to remove this interruption by folding that other into its process.

This encounter with the "other" should not be confused with the surrounding world. Levinas argues that the otherness of this world remains subject to the "powers"[27] of the ego. The "same" of the ego is capable of consuming and transforming the otherness of the world into its own process of identification. The otherness that is the world can and is reconstituted by the ego or the "same." Levinas describes this encounter with the world in terms of intentionality and enjoyment.[28] The difference between the ego and its world is that the world offers itself to be consumed by the ego. It allows itself to be dissolved into the intentions of the ego.

The true other must be an alterity that cannot be exhaustively comprehended by the work of the ego. This "other" cannot be reduced to the intentionality of the ego; it retains a remnant that cannot be folded into the work of this ego. The phenomenological distinction between these two types of otherness is predicated on the capacity for language or discourse. The other person remains an alterity to the work of the ego because it is through conversation that this relation exists. Conversation marks the distance between the same and the other because it forces the ego (the same) to "justify" itself before the other.[29] The encounter between the "same" and the "other," which is glimpsed in the conversation, indicates genuine irreducible otherness because the ego must respond; the ego is compelled to speak to the other.

The dialogue between the same and the other is not initially predicated on the work of ontology. To be sure, the ego seeks to possess the other in terms of intelligibility, but the very possibility of possession is based on the

26. Ibid., 37.
27. Ibid., 38.
28. Ibid., 109–21; see also Levinas, *Existence and Existents*, 27–44.
29. Ibid., 40.

more primordial encounter between them. Levinas argues that without the reality of this primordial encounter the very necessity for thought and language would not appear. The gap between the same and the other produces the possibility of thought and language. The other person places a demand on the ego to make "apology" for itself; "the very fact of being in a conversation consists in recognizing in the Other a *right* over this egoism."[30] The ever-present distance makes communication possible and necessary. Sociality, the relationship between the same and the other, a relationship that cannot be exhaustively calculated, marks the distance between the same and the other. Levinas points to the impossibility of totally comprehending this distance as the phenomenological proof of transcendence.

Ontology, however, seeks to evaporate this distance—to bring it under the domain of knowledge. The ontological operation is the attempt to corral alterity into its framework. This effort is produced by reducing the relation of the other and the same into a "middle term." At first glance, the operation of ontology appears to keep the distance intact. The modality of theoretical reflection—ontology—"designates first a relation with being such that the knowing being lets the known being manifest itself while respecting its alterity and without marking it in any way whatever by this cognition."[31] The reduction of the other into the same appears to be a false claim because the first move of reflective comprehension is to allow the other to manifest itself as other. The reduction occurs through the subtle but powerful way that reflective thought puts into place a horizon of meaning or comprehension. In other words, the work of ontology begins by constructing a framework wherein the encounter between the same and the other can be comprehended. This framework acts as the "middle term" that turns the conversation into a discourse.

Levinas, in his work *Otherwise Than Being*,[32] furthers his case by arguing that ontological thinking attempts to reverse the order between dialogue and discursive thought. One of the premier themes of this later work is the difference between "the saying" and "the said."[33] "The saying" operates much like "the Other" in *Totality and Infinity*. It is representative of the encounter between the same and the other; it names the modality or approach that constitutes the very fact of language. "The said," however,

30. Ibid., 40.
31. Ibid., 42.
32. Levinas, *Otherwise Than Being*.
33. Ibid., 5–7; 37–38; 45–60; 153–61.

is the work of ontology. Like the relationship between the same and the other where ontology seeks to evaporate the transcendent distance, the said is a movement where the act of speaking is reduced to what is said. The significance is shifted from the act of speaking to what is said. Levinas believes that the ethical import of this primordial unbridgeable relationship between the same and the other is forgotten because it is transformed into a discourse where the encounter is contained and given its exhaustive meaning.

The inversion of the process is further clarified by relating knowledge to the concept of light. The theoretical framework serves like a light in that it illuminates the room prior to entering. Prior to the encounter, the light will make known what will take place. This predetermination is a light; it is a horizon of meaning upon which the movement of the other is made possible.[34] Meaning is established by ontology. Ontology is the capacity to lay out a horizon whereby the encounter takes place. The possession of a theoretical construct makes knowledge possible because it serves as the primary condition for the process of knowing. Ontology erects a structure of meaning that sets the standard for determining what will count as knowledge or truth. This is the movement of ontology to invert the priority of the encounter between two people underneath the effort to establish a comprehensive epistemological framework. The alterity of the other person is reduced to the signification prescribed by the framework of knowledge: "in it the shock of the encounter of the same with the other is deadened."[35]

The prioritization of ontology carries numerous problems. One of the chief consequences of this programmatic endeavor is its reduction of the singularity of the other person. Levinas describes this movement as the turning of the other into a concept. Ontology works against the independence of the other person by determining where he/she fits in the conceptual framework. "For the things the work of ontology consists in apprehending the individual (which alone exists) not in his individuality but in its generality (of which there alone is science)."[36] The individuality of the person that approaches is set aside for the more important agenda of categorizing and assigning him/her to the general framework. A comment by Levinas illuminates the movement to turn the other into a concept and its ethical implications.

34. Levinas, *Totality and Infinity*, 44.
35. Ibid., 42.
36. Ibid., 44.

> In relation to beings in the opening of being, comprehension finds signification for them on the basis of being. In this sense, it does not invoke these beings but only names them, thus accomplishing a violence and a negation…partial negation, which is violence, denies the independence of a being: it belongs to me. Possession is the mode whereby a being, while existing, is partially denied.[37]

The effort embedded in the prioritization of ontology over encounter creates this movement where the person I encounter is transformed into a name. The result of this is to "deny" the "independence" of the person I encounter. I have reduced him/her to a theme. This reduction is a violent grasping of the other person. I have turned him/her into something that can be used or consumed. The construction of Western philosophy, then, is consumptive; it pursues an unchecked desire for knowledge at the cost of its responsibility toward the other person.[38] Ontology seeks to reduce the alterity of the other person into something that can be used or consumed through the freedom of the same.

This modality of possession deepens the danger of ontology because it does violence to the other person. This violence, which is not always physical, is the reduction of that person to a theme. One of Levinas' most penetrating analyses of the violent nature of ontology is located in his article "Freedom and Command."[39] Levinas argues that the violence of ontology is inscribed in the way that ontology works to come at a person "indirectly."[40] This violence is described as an "ambush" in that one attempts to fit the other person into a system of "logistics and calculations." For Levinas, the violence inflicted by ontology is violent long before any actual action is taken against the other. The move to absorb this other person into a system of thought is to rob him/her of his/her individuality; it is to turn them into a concept. Violence is already enacted in this conceptualizing move because that which might counter or critique this violence, that which might stay the hand, is shut off and silenced. Levinas describes this violence as an act to view the other person "in the third person, hidden by that which represents it."[41] The person is dissolved into the network of the ontological

---

37. Levinas, "Is Ontology Fundamental?" in *Emmanuel Levinas*, 9.
38. Levinas, *Totality and Infinity*, 46.
39. Levinas, "Freedom and Command" in *Collected Philosophical Papers*, 15–23.
40. Ibid., 19.
41. Ibid., 20.

system. The person becomes a thing, a theme within the overarching system of knowledge.

The end result of this prioritization is the implementation of a pattern of thought and action which fails to achieve its desired goals. The heart of this trajectory is to bring about peace. One of the chief ends for ontological reasoning is to move the world into a peaceful coexistence. The comprehensive framework is an effort to establish harmony amongst the difference of existence. Levinas' article "Peace and Proximity"[42] illuminates the limitations of this effort toward peace. Levinas argues that this effort to bring about peace is a "peace on the basis of truth."[43] The crux of this effort is to establish a conceptual framework where "the diverse agrees with itself and unites…where the other is reconciled with the identity of the identical in everyone."[44] Ontology is the work of peace, then, because it is the conceptual framework that enables this assimilation to take place. The achievement of peace is founded in the act of bringing the variety of people under one banner, which relieves the tension embedded in their differences. Levinas points out, however, that even with this dignified effort such peace has yet to be achieved. In fact, Levinas argues, the opposite has more often been the case.

> This history of peace, freedom, and well-being promised on the basis of a light projected by a universal knowledge on the world and human society—and even on religious teachings that seek justification in the truths of knowledge—this history does not recognize itself in the millennia of fratricidal, political, and bloody struggles, of imperialism, of human hatred and exploitation, up to our century of world wars, genocides, the Holocaust, and terrorism; of unemployment, the continuing poverty of the Third World; of the pitiless doctrines and cruelties of fascism and National Socialism, up to the supreme paradox where the defense of the human and its rights is inverted into Stalinism.[45]

The effort to locate the one viewpoint or horizon from which all of existence can be organized and explained has resulted in this litany of horrors. The desire for peace, this noble and dignified desire, is thwarted by

---

42. Levinas, "Peace and Proximity" in *Emmanuel Levinas*, 161–69.
43. Ibid., 162.
44. Ibid., 162.
45. Ibid., 163.

the very effort to bring it about. Peace is elusive; assimilation fails to bring about its desired goal.

The nature of this violence is more severe because it is attached to the noble goal of achieving peace. The problem is not the desire for peace, but the strategy for achieving that end. The effort to unify the variations of people and things in terms of a single conceptual scheme has, unfortunately, exacerbated the very violence it seeks to overcome. Peace cannot be achieved from this direction because it must employ violence to suppress the distance between people. Levinas describes this as the attempt to eliminate the "proximity" between people. Ontology works to eliminate the differences and distances between people as its pathway toward peace. Peace, according to ontology, is an agreement or a coincidence. Unity is sought through the elimination of difference. This is a doomed project, according to Levinas, because the reality of alterity continues to resurface. Levinas argues that even though one can certainly kill the other person or reduce them to a conceptual scheme this alterity is never fully vanquished. The alterity between the one and the other is of a different order altogether: it is ethical and not ontological. As Levinas states "the infinite paralyses power by its infinite resistance to murder, which, firm and insurmountable, gleams in the face of the Other."[46] In other words, although one can reduce the other person to a scheme or annihilate him/her altogether it is impossible to remove this alterity or ethical order. The otherness of the other person will continue to crop up. The distance between the one and the other, which is seemingly removed by the work of "murdering" knowledge, remains intact—the ethical demand of the other, which is embedded in his/her alterity, remains in effect even after the work of unification has taken place. The attempt to fill in the distance is a futile effort—this proximity cannot be eradicated either through murder or through ontology. Peace through assimilation is no peace at all. It is a failure because it overlooks the basic condition for existence—namely, alterity or proximity. The attempt to eliminate the distance between persons cannot be accomplished, according to Levinas, because alterity is etched into the framework of the universe. This inability to finally remove alterity leads to frustration which can lead to a redoubled effort of removing that distance. Violence flourishes because one must continually work harder and harder at making the proverbial square peg fit into the round hole.

---

46. Levinas, *Totality and Infinity*.

The Trace of the Face in the Politics of Jesus

Levinas criticizes ontology because it fails to support and maintain the infinite distance between persons. The ontological endeavor is to implement a conceptual framework that will exhaustively describe reality thereby erasing that distance. The achievement of this description furthers the agenda for peace by constructing a framework of unity—all differences are submerged into that unifying construct. The face to face encounter, which for Levinas underscores all of existence, is subordinated to the more important effort of naming and articulating that relationship. The distance between the one and the other is seemingly calculated and explained. The desire for peace, however, is frustrated because this infinite distance cannot be comprehended. The frustration spills over as the other is viewed as an opposition to this effort, as a willing resistance against peace. Violence, then, is viewed as a necessary work for bringing these unwilling elements to unification. The proverbial round hole is cut or extended to allow a better fit with the square peg or the square peg is hammered into the round hole. In either case, the peace to be achieved is produced by the manipulation of the other. The ontological framework takes priority even over the life of the other.

The Face of the Other

Levinas' discussion of the face is an outgrowth of his critique of ontology. The face stands as the event that defies the ontological endeavor. The face is the phenomenon of alterity. Drawing from his discussion regarding ontological thinking, Levinas argues that even though we are capable of killing one another we are incapable of finally removing the alterity of the other; in other words, the reality that the face expresses does not disappear in the act of murder. The effort to kill the other is an effort to remove this reality. The violence of ontology is described as an attempt to come at the other person at an angle, i.e., to turn the other into a theme or concept where the face of the other is reduced and avoided: "I have not looked at him in the face, I have not encountered his face . . . To be in relation with the other face to face is to be unable to kill."[47] The point that Levinas intends to make is that the face and all that it expresses precedes the work of ontology. Truth and knowledge are not viewed as the origins of this existence. Human community, which is expressed in the face, becomes the heart and context for the development of truth and knowledge. The attempt to kill the other person

47. Levinas, "Is Ontology Fundamental?" in *Emmanuel Levinas*, 9.

The Kenotic Bridge

can be fulfilled, but it is unable to destroy the order of which the face of the other person articulates—alterity remains even after one is killed.

The violence enacted to remove alterity is a violence that seeks to implement peace by reducing distance and difference. In "Freedom and Command,"[48] Levinas wrestles with the Western philosophical tradition's preoccupation with tyranny. One of the basic issues that this tradition has grappled with is how action, i.e., a command to another, can coexist with freedom, i.e., the one who is commanded. The solution to this problem has been the discovery that both the will of the commander and the subject are coordinated in human rationality; i.e., the command given does not breach the freedom of the commanded because he/she recognizes this command as "reasonable."[49] Tyranny, then, arises in two ways. First, rationality, in its splendor, remains embedded in the human body with all of its passions and emotions. Human rationality remains subject to an abduction where the command to the other is predicated not in rational thought but in the animalistic passions. This amounts to a tyranny of the senses where desire hijacks the movement of reason and asserts commands through whims. The second way is brought about by the passage of time. Here the problem is not an abduction but the inability to recognize the justification or ground for the reasons that coordinate the commander and commanded: "Institutions obey a rational order in which freedom no longer recognizes itself."[50] The reason for doing what is commanded no longer makes sense. The world has moved on from the original discussion. This changes the dynamic between the commanded and the commander. In both cases tyranny arises and destroys the solution. The failure, according to Levinas, is not predicated on the lack of a conceptual scheme or strategy; the history of the Western philosophical tradition is replete with great minds. The failure is buried in the forgetfulness of the human community which preceded the move to implement a rational order. The face of the other constantly communicates this priority of alterity as the basis of rational thought. Tyranny has already been thwarted in the encounter which precedes the decision to register an impersonal rational order to govern human existence.

> It is perhaps this persuasion, this reason prior to reason, that makes coherent discourse and impersonal reason human. Before placing themselves in an impersonal reason, *is it not necessary that*

---

48. Levinas, "Freedom and Command" in *Collected Philosophical Papers*, 15–23.
49. Ibid., 15.
50. Ibid., 17.

> *different freedoms be able to freely understand one another without this understanding being already present in the midst of reason?*[51]

What is forgotten is that a conversation, an encounter between people, preceded the discussion about implementing the rational order. A dialogue precedes the discussion about what will match the will of the commander and the will of the commanded. Prior to the work of comprehension stands the order of the face. The ontological endeavor is constituted by this encounter.

Levinas returns to the discussion of language for helping to develop the order instituted by the face. The alterity between the one and the other and its priority is also embedded in the act of speaking. Levinas contrasts the order that follows the notion of vision (ontology) with the order that follows the notion of speaking (sociality). He combats the assumption that prior to speaking we "see" the other person whereby the priority of ontological reasoning is instituted over against ethical responsibility. The Western philosophical tradition has postulated that vision is the primary posture toward the world and therefore, the relationship between the one and the other falls under its domain. The face, however, refuses to be contained[52] by the vision of intentionality. The other person does not present him/herself as an object for my enjoyment: he/she speaks to me. The very possibility of vision and comprehension of the other is founded on the fact that he/she approaches me—"the movement proceeds from the other."[53] Language, then, is the articulation of this approach; "In discourse the divergence that inevitably opens between the Other as my theme and the Other as my interlocutor . . . forthwith contests the meaning I ascribe to my interlocutor."[54] The encounter between the one and the other is grounded on the fact of their conversation. The approach embedded within language makes meaning possible while simultaneously contesting "the meaning I ascribe." The sound and directionality of his/her voice breaks apart the conceptualizing theme I encase him/her with; "I have neglected the universal being that he incarnates in order to remain with the particular being he is."[55]

---

51. Ibid., 18.
52. Levinas, *Totality and Infinity*, 194.
53. Ibid., 196.
54. Ibid., 195.
55. Levinas, "Is Ontology Fundamental?" in *Emmanuel Levinas*, 7.

The Kenotic Bridge

Turning to *Otherwise Than Being*[56] we find this argument deepened by Levinas' distinction between "the saying and the said." Levinas argues that the act of speaking signifies two important elements. First, it is the foundation for what he calls the said; i.e., the act of speaking makes discursive reasoning possible. Levinas does not attempt to demolish ontological thinking but rather to indicate its conditioned nature. The second signification, however, is this approach to the other which he terms "proximity."[57] Proximity is an act of approach—a conversation. Levinas articulates it this way.

> It [saying] imprints its trace on the thematization itself, which hesitates between, on the one hand, structuration, order of a configuration of entities, world and history for historiographers and, on the other hand, the order of non-nominalized apophansis of the other, in which the said remains a *proposition*, a proposition made to a neighbor, "a signifyingness dealt" to the other.[58]

The act of speaking to a person is necessary for discursive reasoning. Levinas, however, argues here that within discursive reasoning a "trace" of this act of speaking avoids being reduced to the conceptual work of discursive reasoning. This trace points away from reasoning to the very encounter that provoked the possibility for such reasoning. Levinas illuminates that the priority placed on words and meanings fails to appreciate what initiated this material in the first place—two people coming together and speaking. Language, the very act of speaking, allows itself to be contained in the said, but it is not exhaustively contained. The very act of speaking is also the portal whereby one glimpses what made the said possible at all. The act of speaking, of which the face of the other expresses, articulates a different starting point for the Western philosophical tradition: ethics precedes ontology.

The ethical nature of this alterity is encased in the face as it approaches the ego through language. The "divergence" between the I and the other is an ethical separation: "it puts the I in question."[59] Levinas' aim is to describe the ethical implications of the other's approach toward the ego. In other words, this approach places the ego into question because it does not originate from the ego: the other appears as infinitely other, he/she is irreducible

---

56. Levinas, *Otherwise Than Being*, 45–59.
57. Ibid., 46.
58. Ibid., 47.
59. Levinas, *Totality and Infinity*, 195.

to the intentionality of the ego. He is quick to explain that this encounter or "epiphany" is not a contestation of wills. It is an invitation "to a relation incommensurate with a power exercised, be it enjoyment or knowledge."[60] This encounter with the other, which is expressed through the face, is not an annihilation of the ego. This relationship is not founded in a contestation between two selves. The power of the ego is not canceled out. "The expression the face introduces into the world does not defy the feebleness of my powers, but my ability for power."[61] In this comment, Levinas points out that the interaction between the ego and the face of the other is not predicated on an attempt by the other to look for a weakness in the ego's intentionality. The face calls the ego's intentionality to responsibility but does not eliminate it. She does not strip me of its use but commands me to use it well.

Otherwise Than Being describes this in terms of "exposure." The ego is exposed to the other and this obligation; it is placed onto the ego. Before the ego can thematize the other, before he/she can bring the other into his/her intentional horizon, the ego is placed under a command or ethical imperative. He/She is called to a responsibility for the other and this responsibility originates in the approach of the other toward the ego—it is not intentional.

> The passivity of exposure responds to an assignation that identifies me as the unique one, not by reducing me to myself, but by stripping me of every identical quiddity, and thus of all form, all investiture, which would slip into the assignation.[62]

Exposure designates that this experience of responsibility and expectation arrive from outside of my intentionality. The I is "assigned" to take care of the other and this "assignation" does not demolish the self, but rather summons it to be responsible. The other calls me forth to be responsible and I am incapable of producing (or eliminating) this call to expectation. "Preexisting the disclosure of being in general taken as a basis of knowledge and as meaning of being is the relation with the existent that expresses himself; preexisting the plane of ontology is the ethical plane."[63] Exposure and assignation indicate the lack of intentionality. Responsibility arises from outside of the ego.

---

60. Ibid., 198.
61. Ibid.
62. Levinas, *Otherwise Than Being*, 49.
63. Levinas, *Totality and Infinity*, 201.

Levinas further describes this as a passivity beyond all passivity. The call of responsibility is not created through one's own conscious effort. Responsibility is placed onto the ego by the encounter with the other person. The call is, then, a summons addressed to the ego. This summons is an inexhaustible call. One of Levinas' chief arguments for this inexhaustible nature is located in his assertion that "the-one-for-the-other" is not a commitment.[64] In other words, not only does this responsibility arise outside of the ego it is also insurmountable: one can never fully grasp its breadth. Responsibility for the other is inexhaustible because it can never be completely turned into an intention: consciousness never fully recovers from this call, it is always under orders. The end result is that the face of the other indicates the irreducible difference between the same and the other while also placing an ethical responsibility onto the same. The fact that language is the ground for ontology, which is captured in the phenomenological experience of the face of the other, means that ethics has priority over comprehension. As was the case with the relationship between the other and the ego so to is the relationship between ethics and ontology. Ethics does not demolish or remove vision, but rather it constitutes it by calling it forth. The key to remember is that this call is a call of responsibility. Ontology is put into the service of ethics, not the other way around.

The heart of human existence, then, is not the determination of truth, but rather the experience of hospitality and sociality. "The object of the encounter is at once given to us and in *society* with us; but we cannot reduce this event of sociality to some property revealed in the given, and knowledge cannot take precedence over sociality."[65] The face indicates an order that precedes and overflows our desire to comprehend. The very possibility for comprehension is founded on the fact that we are in relation—the fact that we live in communities. Certainly, one can begin to calculate and figure the angles of this or that community, but one never fully reduces that experience of the one to the other in those terms. Levinas' instructs his readers to remember their responsibility as they employ the ontological machinery. Prior to the use of our powers of comprehension there is the call to use it well. Sociality and ethics precede the thirst for knowledge and the face invokes one to remember that orientation toward existence.

---

64. Levinas, *Otherwise Than Being*, 136–40.
65. Levinas, "Is Ontology Fundamental?" in *Emmanuel Levinas*, 8.

The Trace of the Face in the Politics of Jesus

Kenosis: The Bridge Between Levinas and Yoder

This project has been working towards the claim that Yoder's work can be reread as containing an underlying philosophy of otherness and that this helps to clarify his work. The problem, however, is that one must demonstrate why such a link is viable. The work to establish Levinas as a dialogue partner in contrast to Huebner's rejection initiated this move toward viability, but it did not secure a basis for why Levinas should be in conversation with Yoder in the first place. There is, however, something that each author has discussed, albeit in different ways, that bridges their differences: kenosis.

The idea of "self-emptying," has been a theme for both authors. Levinas' material on kenosis is not large, but it does appear as a theme he considered to be in connection with his work on otherness.[66] Certainly Levinas' discussions of this concept are very carefully crafted and remain committed to his understanding of Judaism. Nonetheless, he does make a case that under certain conditions this line of thinking can be a way of pointing to the importance of otherness. For Yoder, though, this theme is prominent for identifying and describing the nature of the politics of Jesus. In fact, the final and culminating chapter of his *Politics* contains an explicit link between the hymnic references of Philippians 2.5–11 and his discussion of the true marks of Christian discipleship.[67] The fact that each thinker has discussed this issue should in no way be understood as an attempt to reduce either thinker into the work of the other. Nonetheless, the commonality of this discussion merits a closer inspection, especially as it serves to create a context for dialogue between them.

Understanding Levinas' discussion of kenosis must proceed only after one fully understands some of his caveats regarding that discussion. First, it is imperative that one recognize that the idea of God's act of self-emptying is not limited to Christianity. The roundtable discussion recorded in *Is It Righteous To Be?* finds Levinas making the case that kenosis can be located in Judaism as well. In fact he goes so far as to say that a parallel can be drawn between these two religions based on this theme.[68] What remains, however, is the importance of recognizing this idea as being broader than Christian

---

66. Two explicit locations are the interview "Judaism and Christianity after Franz Rosenzweig" in *Is It Righteous To Be?* and his article "A Man-God?" in *Entre Nous*, 53–60.

67. Yoder, *Politics of Jesus*, 228–47 (233–37).

68. Levinas, "Judaism and Christianity after Franz Rosenzweig" in *Is It Righteous To Be?*, 257.

The Kenotic Bridge

theology. Second, and maybe even more important, is his caution to allow kenosis to become a meaning bearing theme for suffering. Throughout this same interview, Levinas is quick to remind his Christian interlocutors of the suffering embedded in Christianity's relationship with Judaism, which culminates in the Holocaust. In particular, Levinas is worried about how Christians have used kenosis as a way of squeezing meaning out of suffering and championing "defenselessness" or inactivity as the way of Christ.[69] In other words, Christians have utilized this concept as a way of keeping oppressed persons from resisting their oppression because it is their service to God or it is a concept which allows Christians to remain inactive while their neighbors are being tyrannized. In either case, the idea of kenosis can easily become complicit with the evils of the historical relationship between Christianity and Judaism.

Even with these cautions, however, Levinas is still able to make a case that kenosis can point to one's responsibility to the other. Levinas' article, "A Man-God?,"[70] makes the case that the descent of God into humanity serves both as a manifestation (albeit as a "trace") of transcendence and as a demonstration of the ethic of substitution. According to Levinas, the descent of God to humanity is a work of humility. This humility "disturbs" the ontological work of reason because it fails to participate in the great endeavor of searching for a meaning. This resistance to meaning is embedded in the approach. It is "allied with the vanquished, the poor, the persecuted" and this is why it resists being caught up in the machinations of ontological thinking.[71] In order to understand what Levinas is after here one can turn to his article "Is Ontology Fundamental?."[72] During his argument about the phenomenological significance of the act of speaking, Levinas states "I have spoken to him, that is to say, I have neglected the universal being that he incarnates in order to remain with the particular being he is."[73] The idea of kenosis is predicated on this humility which disturbs the work of ontology. The idea that God aligns with "the vanquished, the poor, the persecuted," is a modality that remains with the particular at the cost of the universal—it is to fly in the face of the ontological move to reduce these particular beings into a larger whole. The humiliation embedded in kenosis points to

---

69. Ibid., 259–60.
70. Levinas, "A Man-God?" in *Entre Nous*, 53–60.
71. Ibid., 55.
72. Levinas, "Is Ontology Fundamental?" in *Emmanuel Levinas*, 1–10.
73. Ibid., 7.

otherness. It manifests an order that contests the order implemented by ontological reasoning.

For Levinas, this otherness that the humiliation of kenosis posits indicates the idea of proximity: it is a relationship. The face of the other, therefore, communicates the priority of one's responsibility which is manifested in this humiliation. The fact that one is responsible for the other prior to reducing that responsibility to an ethical system is parallel with the responsibility expressed in the alignment of God with human beings: kenosis, self-emptying, is another way of coming at the priority of the other and one's ethical responsibility for taking care. The portrayal of the divine descending into humanity posits a parallel argument for transcendence in that it is an event that cannot be recuperated and calculated. This inability to recalibrate is likened to the face of the other as it turns toward me. I am put into question and accused by the other's turn toward me. One is taught not how to place this other into categories and calculations, but that one must serve him/her. Kenosis communicates the priority of ethics because God aligns God's self with the particular.

Yoder's assessment of kenosis is similar in that Yoder is interested in the ethical rather than the metaphysical nature of this act of self-emptying. In fact, Yoder believes that the most basic understanding of this idea is not the ontological implications of what it means for God to incarnate Godself in a human being, but rather that this act carries within it a moral and political vision. In other words, what is significant about kenosis is not the underlying substantive claims of Christians, but the kind of posture or approach to the world that it demands. Yoder compares this act with the story of the fall of humanity in Genesis 3.[74] This does not mean that the Philippians 2[75] passage does not speak to the idea of a divine condescension, but that its primary focus is to instantiate an ethical posture of which Christians are to model. Yoder argues that this text points to Adam and Eve's inability to be satisfied with their human nature. Genesis 3 is the story of human beings reaching out to make God's power and prestige their own. The result of this is an ethic of power grabbing; it is a posture of seizure and control. Philippians 2, however, is the story of Jesus' temptation to reenact this failure and his success in refusing its seductive qualities. In other words, Yoder argues

---

74. I am drawing the bulk of my material from Yoder's meditation on Philippians 2 located in *He Came Preaching Peace*, 89–95.

75. Philippians 2.5–8.

that the kenosis, exemplified by Jesus, is the instantiation of an alternative form of ethics: it is the politics of servanthood and peace.

Yoder goes on to show that the passage's attributing divinity to Jesus is not merely to express some doctrinal point, but rather to demonstrate that this type of ethical posture is also the character of God: "The creator of the universe is a servant."[76] This character and nature of God as servant is, for Yoder, exemplified by a posture of service toward others. Kenosis communicates an alternative understanding of subjectivity wherein the dignity of the other, including the enemy other, becomes the mark of God's being. The politics of Jesus, then, are founded on the willingness to sacrifice effectiveness for obedience. Yoder argues that kenosis is a demonstration of this deep level commitment to the dignity of the other person, even the enemy other. It is a commitment to this other even at the cost of being effective or making sense. Effectiveness is not eschewed because Yoder thinks it is evil, it is eschewed because it always reduces the other person to a conceptual system which can, and often does, justify violent behavior toward one's neighbor (friend or foe). Christians are called to embody the politics of Jesus and this embodiment must take on the character of God's kenosis.

Rereading Yoder on Methodology and Revolutionary Subordination

The idea of kenosis, which is the baseline content of Yoder's articulation of the politics of Jesus, can be used to make the connection with Levinas' work on otherness. Levinas' idea that kenosis is another way of coming at the issue of otherness can be incorporated to help illuminate a deep commitment to otherness embedded in Yoder's work. This consideration of otherness, then, becomes another way of grounding Yoder's material. On the surface, to be sure, Yoder believes that the call to follow Jesus is answered because one aligns oneself with him. Yoder does not offer the idea of otherness as a proof for accepting and embodying the politics of Jesus. One is a disciple because one has chosen to follow Jesus. This choice to follow leads to the effort to model his/her life after Jesus. Nonetheless, in order to help clarify his position, especially to those who may not be convinced, one is able to reach for this argument concerning otherness to help make his point. The key for him is that the argument serves to turn the attention of the interlocutor back onto the example of Jesus; in other words, the translation of the

76. Yoder, *He Came Preaching* Peace, 93.

The Trace of the Face in the Politics of Jesus

politics of Jesus into a commitment to otherness is not aimed at eliminating Jesus as the central source for these politics. To do so would be to take the road of effectiveness. The idea here is to redefine effectiveness; i.e. being effective is not measured by how many are convinced but by the ability of the argument to continue to maintain the notion, within the Church's ever shifting context, that Jesus is Lord.

Yoder's wariness of methodological work, then, can be viewed as an extension of this commitment to otherness. The idea of dialogue is a paramount feature in Yoder's work. This is proved by Yoder's choice to mainly write in an essay format. At every point Yoder envisioned his work as a conversation; essays were more conducive to dialogue because they did not immediately rule interlocutors out at the outset. The heart of his critique of methodologism is its penchant for locating that fundamental set of principles or processes whereby the conversation could be initiated. Yoder, in terms of Christian theological and moral discourse, likened methodologism to idolatry because that work presumed "the right to set the terms under which God can be recognized."[77] This criticism can be broadened in that methodologism at any level takes onto itself that right to determine the parameters and interlocutors that will be involved. Methodologism, then, stifles conversations by removing interesting insights and interlocutors thereby limiting the potentiality of the discourse.

Levinas' notion that ontology forgets or overlooks the fact that human community and interaction are its foundation is parallel to Yoder's recognition that methodologism also forgets how human communities have previously developed a numerous and divergent set of reasons for deliberating moral issues. Levinas and Yoder agree that these efforts overlook the fact that human experience precedes them. What is lacking in Yoder is a further development of this important reality. Levinas goes further by illuminating the importance of this human community as the very source of ontological reasoning. Not only does Levinas further develop this otherness as the structure of human existence he also illuminates how ontology seeks to overlook it. Ontology is always seeking to recuperate what is other into its comprehensive system. Otherness is something to be overcome.

Methodologism works similarly in that it operates under the impression that the best way to have a conversation is by getting all of the participants to agree beforehand how the conversation ought to take place.

---

77. Yoder, "Walk and Word: The Alternatives to Methodologism" in *Theology Without Foundations*, 89.

The Kenotic Bridge

Reflecting back on Yoder's discussion of methodologism, one is able to view the problems in terms of a dismissal of otherness.[78] The search for the proper first principles, the insertion of theory over human experience, and the demand that local communities re-identify themselves in terms of a larger, universal language all point to a loss of otherness. Methodologism is a reduction of otherness into a currently held larger whole that serves as the frame of absolute truth. This move is destructive of conversation because it monopolizes the dialogue. Yoder's problem with Gustafson's call for him to translate his work into philosophical categories is that it is a call to eliminate its particular aspects; in other words, Yoder's particular commitments and ideas have to be reshaped and transformed in order for him to participate in the discussion. Yoder is allowed to come to the dance, but only if he looks and acts like those who are already there. The otherness of Yoder's perspective is eclipsed by being reduced to the comprehensive scheme, which controls the conversation. Methodologism seeks to remove all otherness. It is parallel to the movement of ontology which seeks to secure a unified comprehensive scheme wherein otherness must be reduced to the larger whole.

Whereas Yoder's critique of methodologism is a negative aspect of this underlying commitment to otherness, his call for revolutionary subordination is a positive directive. It is positive in that it calls Christians to actively engage their surroundings. The idea that one is to voluntarily subordinate him/herself to his/her interlocutors is predicated on what Yoder calls the dignity of the other person, even if he/she is our enemy. The dignity of the other person is an important element throughout Yoder's work. It is similarly derived from Jesus self-emptying political model spoken of above. The other person, even if he/she is an enemy, possesses dignity and Jesus did not sacrifice this for the sake of a larger cause or justification. He voluntarily subordinated himself to their power and in so doing demonstrated a commitment to their dignity as human beings. This notion of dignity is easily linked with Levinas' conception of otherness, especially the face, because it instantiates the reality of the other person as well as an ethical order that commands a certain kind of orientation toward this genuine other.

Although Yoder's description of revolutionary subordination is primarily an attempt to demonstrate the earliest Christian community's capacity for moral reasoning, he also articulates some of the motivations and aims of this particular practice. Through his effort to distinguish the

---

78. Cf. ch. 1.

Christian conduct codes from Stoicism one discovers some of the contours that motivate and direct this practice. One of his first distinctions is the way in which Stoic codes are aimed at developing one's personal character. The relational structure of existence, or the plight of the other person, is merely a context wherein one is able to build up, through moral conduct, his/her character. Revolutionary subordination, however, is aimed at establishing and maintaining relationships. Community, not personal development, is the primary concern of these Christian conduct codes. This emphasis on relationality points back to Levinas' argument that the face of the other instantiates a reality where both the "same" and the "other" exist. This relationality points to a world founded on otherness rather than a self-projected existence. The codes are aimed at maintaining this reality; a reality that is inscribed in the face of the other.

Another aspect of this practice is the way in which its evaluative basis is predicated on the relationship to the other. In other words, revolutionary subordination is a practice aimed at the plight of the other. The Stoic codes are aimed at personal development and growth. The relationship and the other are merely a construct or frame used by the subject to better his/her character. The plight of the other is only important as it relates to one's own personal goals; whatever help that one might give is first predicated on what one will receive by helping (Yoder describes this view as a "detachment"). Revolutionary subordination inverts this self-centered perspective by centering on the other person and the relationship. Hearkening back to Yoder's argument that the tower of Babel story[79] indicates that God opts for plurality rather than singularity, one can easily see that the stoic codes, with their emphasis on the self, are aimed at instituting a more monotonous and controlled universe. Revolutionary subordination cultivates a vision aimed toward plurality. The net result of this fact is its interconnection with Levinas' argument that the face of the other points to a proximity or irreducible separation between the same and the other. Revolutionary subordination is a set of conduct codes that seeks to maintain this irreducible relation. Revolutionary subordination instantiates that moral judgment is grounded on the maintenance of relationships; relationality is the field for evaluating moral experience.

This emphasis on relationality and the other also points to a revision of the notion of subjectivity. Another of Yoder's distinctions is that stoicism is concerned with developing one's own personal moral status; i.e. morality

---

79. Cf. ch. 1.

is a self-creating journey. The only real obligation is to better oneself. Any aid given to the other person is produced only as a means toward self-refinement. This robust notion of subjectivity is dampened by Yoder's call for revolutionary subordination. The impetus for subordination is not for securing a stronger sense of self; instead, it is motivated by service to the other person. His/her subjectivity is the central factor; one is concerned not with oneself but with the other. The subjectivity of revolutionary subordination is described as a subjectivity that is under orders to serve the other person. Another way of viewing this subtle change is to recognize that these codes are meant for everyone. No one is exempt from this obligation to serve the other person. Stoicism sought to delineate not only when one submits him/herself but also who is to be taken care of and who is to be avoided. These caveats are disregarded by the Haustafeln codes: everyone is called on to practice revolutionary subordination. This directly lines up with Levinas' notion of subjectivity. One's subjectivity is founded in and through the other person. This given subjectivity comes also with a moral responsibility. For Levinas this means that one is under obligation to the other even before one is able to choose—the passivity beyond all passivity. In other words, human beings, according to Levinas, are not able to choose whether they will view themselves as moral beings. Their choice is, rather, whether they will heed the call of the other. Revolutionary subordination contains a parallel view of subjectivity.

The end result is that revolutionary subordination posits a moral responsibility to the other person. To be sure, it is formulated in terms of following Jesus. Nevertheless, it is still evident that a posture toward the other person exists as well. Yoder's call for Christians to subordinate themselves to the order in which they find themselves is an ethical mandate derived from the example of Jesus. Jesus life and teaching testify to the nature of God and this nature can be explicated as a responsibility toward the other person. For Yoder, God is committed to the other person; it is embedded in God's nature. The radical openness of Yoder's work is founded on the conception that God does not force persons to follow. God provides the space necessary for that person to choose to align him/herself with God. This fundamental posture toward the other person surfaces in a practice like revolutionary subordination in that the one who freely subordinates him/herself does so in the full knowledge that they know better, but they do not forcibly impose their knowledge on the other person. God is for the other and so must be his followers.

Conclusion

Summary

THE INITIAL BASIS FOR this work was the idea that John Howard Yoder's thought remains significant for contemporary Christian theological and moral reflection. Drawing its impetus from the invitation issued by Mark Nation, this project sought to align Yoder with Emmanuel Levinas in order to maintain and extend Yoder's relevance. This project was an exploration of an experimental link between these two thinkers. The hope was that Levinas could tease out the deeper contours of Yoder's thought without losing the authenticity of Yoder's purposes. This work argued that Levinas' notion of otherness, especially in his critique of ontology and the description of the phenomenological encounter of the face of the other, was an admirable framework for accomplishing that task. Through a rereading of Yoder's work we were able to see a fundamental orientation of the one-for-the-other underlying Yoder's claims. This posture toward a responsibility to the other person was another way of characterizing the life and thought of Jesus without abandoning Yoder's claim that "Jesus is Lord." The Christian claim that "Jesus is Lord" is characterized as a turning to a lifestyle of service to other persons, regardless of whether they are one's neighbor or enemy. It is a posture founded on the dignity of the other person, a dignity which precedes the ontological effort to understand her.

This project has yielded interesting insights into Yoder's work. We limited ourselves to Yoder's methodology and revolutionary subordination. Levinas' critique of ontology deepened Yoder's suspicions regarding methodologism. The point is not that Yoder believed sloppy work was valuable, but rather that he recognized that too often methodological work sought to transcend the descriptive task by attempting to create normative guidelines for discourse. In a similar way to Levinas' description of the comprehension of the ontological effort, this strategy works to manipulate and conceptualize its context. Each thinker argued that this effort produces a posture of grasping the other person. The threat of violence stands in the shadows of this seizure of power and control. Ontology, like methodologism, is not satisfied with mere description; it is imbued with a lust for power. The link with Levinas enables us to see deeper elements within Yoder's worries about the overemphasis on methodology.

Revolutionary subordination claimed that the newly converted Christians had to subordinate themselves under their current structural context. Yoder believed that in and through this subordination real change could occur. His critics, of course, found this picture wanting. They claimed that Yoder's work would only reinforce the hierarchal patterns of current relational experience. The problem with Yoder is that his call for subordination signaled a retreat from making changes to oppressive relational structures. The application of Levinas' notion of otherness, however, helped to illuminate Yoder's recognition that Jesus' political vision is as concerned with one's enemy as it is concerned with one's neighbor. Yoder was not against seeking changes to current relational structures, but he was certainly concerned with how such changes were brought about. The concept of otherness points out this subtle, but important part of Yoder's idea. The ethical responsibility embedded within Jesus' political vision does not cease when a person faces his enemy. Yoder believed that the responsibility of the Christian to the other person included his enemy. The idea of revolutionary subordination is not primarily geared to refuse change, but it is directed toward finding ways of bringing this change that continues to note and accept the otherness of one's enemy: the human dignity of the oppressor.

The first phase sought to narrow the breadth of Yoder's work to two key elements: his methodological approach and his articulation of the practice of revolutionary subordination. These two elements were significant because they embodied Yoder's portrayal of the Christian life as faithfulness to Jesus. These were viewed because they are significant and controversial. Many of Yoder's critics view these elements as housing the problems of his work. This first phase worked to describe them, highlighting their significance for his work.

The second phase examined the criticisms of his work. The trajectory of this chapter was to articulate the nature of the critiques. It was also concerned with showing that these criticisms could not be written off as being directed from a presupposition that Yoder's work is sectarian. This second point showed that these critiques contained genuine questions and pointed to real limitations of Yoder's work. Looking at the work of James Gustafson, A. James Reimer, and Elisabeth Schüssler Fiorenza this chapter raised these deeper problems and demonstrated the limited nature of Yoder's replies.

The third phase examined the work of three Yoder supporters. These thinkers sought to demonstrate that Yoder's work was not subject to these criticisms by linking Yoder to portions of the Western philosophical tradition. This effort accomplished two key points. First, their efforts served as a validation of my own. It is in and through their work that I was able to undertake this exploratory endeavor. Second, these authors also demonstrated the dangers of such projects. One danger is the cost of losing important purposes of Yoder through that conversation. The answers they provided to his critics were achieved only at the cost of turning Yoder's work into something foreign. Still, their efforts were important for setting the stage for my own.

The final phase demonstrated how a conversation with Emmanuel Levinas could help to refute Yoder's critics while still maintaining a fidelity to his own claims. This step began by showing that Levinas' work was a sufficient conversation partner. From there it moved to delineate those parts of the Levinasian framework that were helpful in teasing out the possibility that an argument of otherness underlay Yoder's corpus. A bridge was built on the concept of *kenosis*. This idea of the condescension of God played a role in both thinkers and it served as a bridge from Levinas' framework to Yoder's material. The politics of Jesus, for Yoder, are tied up with this idea of kenosis; it serves as an interpretive model for Jesus behavior and it is part of what he believes is taking place in revolutionary subordination. This link, then, allowed me to consider the possibility that something like Levinas' ethical conception of otherness could be used to restate Yoder's work without losing connection to Yoder's aims. This chapter showed that restating Yoder in terms of Levinas' notion of otherness was not only possible, but fruitful. The chapter finished highlighting what Yoder's critics had missed in their critiques. The concept of otherness illuminated these deeper aspects and demonstrated the insufficiencies of their readings of Yoder.

The possibilities opened up by this interconnection warrants further studies between these two thinkers. This comparative enterprise illuminated the potential within opening a doorway into uncharted and intriguing areas of study within Yoder's work. The project recognizes that it has only begun the process of extending Yoder beyond his normal boundaries. Predicated on the fact that many other Yoderian scholars have already linked Yoder with some form of the Western philosophical tradition, this project carries this impetus in a new direction that can help to move beyond the problems associated with their work. This project initializes a new direction for Yoderian scholarship. Nevertheless, even with the promise attached to this project certain key issues remain to be discussed. Time constraints have not permitted an extensive examination of some of the remaining issues, but to leave them unmentioned would be shameful. The final portion of this conclusion is dedicated to briefly explicating the contours of these questions and their possible answers.

Abiding Issues

The link between Levinas and Yoder is not without its issues. Due to time constraints, I have chosen to briefly describe them as questions for future study. This section of the paper is not intended to comprehensively answer these questions, but to let the reader know the nature of the continuing questions and some possible avenues of response. I have chosen three questions to look at. My choice of these three questions does not exhaust the questions that could be raised, but I believe that these three are imperative for future work on this topic. The three questions are: 1) Does the link between Yoder and Levinas compromise the central role that Jesus plays in Yoder's thought? 2) Does Levinas' refusal to label himself a pacifist undermine this effort because of Yoder's unswerving commitment to pacifism? 3) Does the connection of these two thinkers only compound the feminist criticisms of their work?

Question One

The nature of this first question has two trajectories. First, the effort to link a Christian ethicist and a Jewish philosopher raises questions regarding the relationship between these two traditions. The basic thrust of this issue is whether one unwittingly reduces one thinker into the tradition of the other; does Levinas' Judaism obscure Yoder's emphasis on Jesus or does Yoder's emphasis on Jesus force an overtly Christian interpretation of Levinas' work? The second trajectory is the question of utilizing a philosophical grid to reread Yoder's work. Throughout this project we have discussed the issue of how to relate Yoder to a philosophical thinker. This was an issue because Yoder believed that linking Christian claims to a philosophical grid could run the risk of reducing those claims to claims of human reason. The particularity of Christianity is lost because its claims become principles of common sense. These two elements are complex and call for a thorough and lengthy treatment. I would like to take the next few moments to better spell out some of the issues associated with each trajectory while also suggesting some possible responses. I will cover the question regarding the relationship between Judaism and Christianity first. I will then move to cover the issue of revelation and natural reason.

The relationship between Judaism and Christianity has been anything but harmonious. Attempting to chart out the contours of this relationship is both large and complex. Only recently, in the dark shadow of the Holocaust, have Christian thinkers made better efforts to understand Judaism in its own terms. The Holocaust and its aftermath have forced Christians to face up to their role in establishing, developing, and employing such a violent pogrom. Christians have come to realize that this tragedy was forged in their deep and lengthy commitment to anti-Semitism and anti-Judaism. The Holocaust was only the culmination of this brewing hatred underlying much Christian thought and practice. The seeds for such an outpouring of violence had been sown long before its physical manifestation. Any effort made to bring about a comparison between Jewish and Christian thinkers must pay heed to this disastrous history as it carefully treads forward.

The danger is that by rereading Yoder through a Levinasian framework one might forget what has taken place historically between Jews and Christians. Attempting to link Yoder and Levinas without paying attention to the historical relationship between Jews and Christians runs the risk of smoothing over real differences and misinterpreting each tradition. There are, however, some reasons for why such a project may actually be helpful for reestablishing a friendlier dialogue between the two traditions. Caution is certainly expected, but it may be that this linkage can open up alternative pathways for this historically negative relationship.

The first way to tackle this question is to repeat the importance that kenosis plays for both authors. Levinas and Yoder both understand kenosis as an integral way of better understanding their work. The differences between Jews and Christians surface here in Levinas' claim that God's condescension can be found in the Hebrew Bible; in other words, Levinas' use of this conception is not limited to its Christian underpinnings—it is Jewish before it is Christian. The similarity between these two in terms of kenosis is further verified by Yoder's insistence to reread Jesus in terms of his Jewish nature. The point is that Yoder would have no trouble extending the notion of kenosis back into the Hebrew scriptures because it helps to strengthen his claim that Jesus was a "Jewish pacifist."[1] The book that contains this assessment is an excellent assortment of essays regarding Yoder's views of Judaism that Michael Cartwright and Peter Ochs have brought together. They are able to show that Yoder sought to engage Jews in terms other than what had gone on before—that is, Yoder believed that a conversation and dialogue could take place by recognizing that the historical relationship between Jews and Christians did not have to go as it did; it was not inevitable. The initial factors of these elements help to support the forward movement of a comparison of Levinas and Yoder because it does not foster the normative relationality between Jews and Christians, but actually might contribute something to move that conversation into a more positive direction.

Yoder believed that Judaism had much to teach Christians about their own tradition, especially about what it meant to be a community in exile. One of the features of this book is Cartwright's description of the friendship that Yoder was able to form with Rabbi Steven S. Schwarzschild.[2] Yoder's efforts to engage Schwarzschild helps to support the view that Yoder believed he could learn from Judaism. What drew Yoder to Schwarzschild was his work locating pacifism within the Talmudic sources. Schwarzschild's work enabled Yoder to better develop his own thinking regarding the nonviolence of Jesus and its relation to Israel's history as recorded in the Hebrew Bible.

A second line of reasoning that Yoder took with regard to Judaism is the idea that Jews had successfully enacted what Christ had called Christians to. The Synagogues and communities of Jews throughout the last two millennia were more in line with a Christian community than Christians were. Basically, Judaism had successfully resisted the temptation to enact a Constantinian approach to life. These Jewish communities worked harder at being faithful to God rather than trying to run the world. According to Yoder, God's message to the prophet Jeremiah, that the Israelites should

---

1. Yoder, "Jesus the Jewish Pacifist" in *Jewish-Christian Schism Revisited*, 69–92.
2. Ibid., 12–19.

seek the peace of the city, became a model for living in exile. This exilic model stands in contrast to Yoder's Constantinian typology because it does not seek to make history come out right. The trajectory of this exilic model is to be faithful to God rather than trying to make all of history conform to God's purpose. According to Yoder, Judaism lived out this model more faithfully than Christians; in fact, part of what moved Christians to adopt the Constantinian model was their efforts to divorce themselves from their Jewish heritage. The tragedies of the relationship between Judaism and Christianity are, in Yoder's mind, based on Christianity's effort to forget its own origins.

Although these elements of Yoder's thought do not comprehensively solve the issues between Jews and Christians, it does offer a willingness to foster a dialogue between the two. Yoder's work stands as an effort to move past the normative standards of engagement; he offers compelling reasons for why this relationship unfolded in the way that it did without justifying those reasons. He clearly states that Christianity's failure to properly model God's purposes by adopting the Constantinian typology had much to do with the violence and destruction enacted on Judaism. Yoder's hope is that Christians will come to realize this failure and begin to rediscover God's purposes for them and in so doing reestablish more peaceful communications with Judaism. Yoder places Christianity in a more vulnerable state by recognizing its own culpability in helping to foster the tragedies it inflicted on Jews throughout history. Yoder was not worried that a conversation with a Jewish thinker would hurt his position as a Christian; instead, Yoder saw it as an opportunity to grow in his own faith.

Still even with these insights and hopes for conversation and dialogue, Peter Ochs points out that there are moments when Yoder continues to be burdened with some of the negative features of this past relationship.[3] There are portions of Israel's history, the monarchy for instance, that do not receive the same kind of attention that Jeremiah's community does. In other words, Yoder's work retains those portions of Judaism that best fit his program while eschewing those that do not. Ochs' comments have two aims. First, this type of characterization of Judaism is the very kind of thing that has taken place throughout its relationship to Christianity. Yoder's anti-monarchical stance already reinscribes the Christian penchant to define its others. Basically, Yoder's ability to strike out the Israelite monarchy

---

3. Ibid., 38–40. Ochs offers a nice summary of the many comments he will provide throughout the book.

period as a form of unfaithfulness is just one more expression of the kind of Christian arrogance that led others to define and harm Jews. This first problematic extends into his second aim. Yoder's anti-monarchical stance contains implications for evaluating Jewish notions of Zionism and the State of Israel. Yoder's elevation of Jeremiah's exilic model over against the period of Jewish sovereignty in the Kingdoms of Israel and Judah implies that contemporary efforts to establish and maintain the nation of Israel are to be judged negatively. Yoder's work contains ingredients that could come together to fuel anti-Zionist movements and Ochs views this as a continuation of the very supersessionism Yoder hoped to overcome. Ochs believes that Yoder's work, while much more exciting and inviting for conversation, continues to allow Christians to predetermine the identity of Judaism in their own terms and to undermine respect for Judaism and its national identity.

Ochs is right to detect a judgment within Yoder's work; he does believe that the monarchical period of Israel's history has been discarded by God. Ochs' fear that Yoder's work will hamper Zionist thinking, however, takes a too simplistic picture of Yoder's criticisms. A closer inspection of Yoder's article regarding Jesus as a Jewish pacifist reveals that Yoder's criticisms of Zionism is not couched in their efforts to form a state, but the fact that they do this in terms of their own power. The Zionism which Yoder seems critical of is a Zionism that too closely identifies itself with the political modes of the surrounding nations rather than through a Jewish centered conception. This kind of critical review of Jewish Zionism is not even limited to Yoder but can be located within Judaism itself.[4] Daniel Boyarin, for example, draws from Yoder's revisionist picture of the history of Jews and Christians in order to buttress his own concerns with contemporary forms of Jewish politics.[5] Boyarin appears most interested in adopting Yoder's call for being political by being outside of the political forms of power—that is, being political through weakness. Boyarin's challenge to Zionist portrayals

---

4. Levinas, a strong supporter of a Jewish State, argues that Israel cannot lose itself by adopting the political policies and practices of the nations around it. This is what he means when he makes "spirituality" a necessary component of Jewish Statehood. Levinas, "Politics After!" in *Levinas Reader*, 277–83. Yoder argues, similarly to Levinas, that when Israel's efforts toward statehood mirror the surrounding nations then it loses its specialized mission and identity from God. See his "Jesus the Jewish Pacifist" in *Jewish-Christian Schism Revisited*, 69–87.

5. Boyarin, "Judaism as a Free Church: Footnotes to John Howard Yoder's *The Jewish-Christian Schism Revisited*," 6–21.

Conclusion

of Israel is rooted in its desire to rule in terms of political strength and power. He argues that Yoder's revisionist history of the Jewish-Christian relationship affords him the possibility to work this out. Determining whether Boyarin's challenges to Jewish Zionism are meritorious extends beyond the scope of this project, but it suffices to show that Yoder's work does not have to be rejected outright. There appears to be an argument within Judaism itself that enables Yoder's work to continue to have import for the Jewish-Christian conversation.

The second part of this original question concerns the effort to link Yoder with a portion of the philosophical tradition. The basic thrust of this question is whether a link between Yoder and Levinas ironically turns Yoder's claims into philosophical propositions. The centrality of Jesus would have been lost because one could have come to the same conclusion without having to reference those claims. We have already looked at Yoder's recognition that Christianity would have to translate its claim that Jesus is lord as it moves through time and space.[6] This act of translation was open to the use of philosophical categories as long as the claims about Jesus were maintained throughout. Yoder pointed to the prologue of John's gospel as a primary example of this type of translation. John's use of the term "logos" was a new vehicle for communicating the message of Jesus, but Jesus was not enveloped by the philosophical framework supporting the notion of "logos;" instead, "logos" was put to work for the Christian message which enabled it to maintain its identity with Jesus while also opening up the story of Jesus beyond its initial borders. The danger of this issue was also abated with Stanley Hauerwas' helpful recognition between the uses of philosophy for explication and validation.[7] Here Hauerwas points to a more nuanced way of understanding the role of philosophy or human reason. The theologian can utilize this material as long as he/she understands that they are merely explicating their content. In other words, philosophy and human reason are essential for clarifying and explaining one's position. Hauerwas believes that Christians can do this because this does not mean that they are trying to prove, on grounds other than their own faith, that God exists. The move to show that God exists outside of Christian claims becomes a move for validation. This type of effort is where Christian claims are turned into something like a philosophical proposition. If one pays attention to

---

6. See Yoder's response to James Gustafson in chapter two, pgs. 57–63.
7. See Stanley Hauerwas' response to Gustafson in chapter three, pgs. 78–80.

what one is attempting to accomplish than one is less likely to fall into this trap.

Another route for buttressing the link between Yoder and philosophy comes from his articulation of middle axioms. The central location of this conception is found in one of Yoder's earliest documents *The Christian Witness to the State*.[8] The basic thrust of this conception is that Christians can and should locate terms for articulating their particular convictions as they engage their surrounding socio-political contexts. The point of these axioms was to foster dialogue between persons of the Christian tradition and their non-Christian neighbors. One of the clearest examples of Yoder employing this conception is his *Body Politics*.[9] Throughout this work Yoder attempts to demonstrate important "sociological" elements within particular Christian practices. His aim is not to ground these practices in something outside of the Christian tradition. Rather, Yoder hopes to show Christians the socio-political aspects of their practices while also teaching them ways they can intelligently articulate their convictions to those outside their communities. The sociological implications of certain practices serve as "middle axioms" for initiating dialogue between the two groups. These factors do not replace the underlying tie to particular Christian convictions, but they do allow for actual dialogue to begin.

These pathways initiate a response from Yoder's side which would allow the use of philosophy. There are within Yoder's work possibilities which would allow and guide such a link. The danger of allowing the philosophical grid to run roughshod over Christian claims remains in place, but the possibility of rereading Yoder's work through it is not inherently doomed.

Coming at this question from Levinas' side we find that his use of phenomenology as the means to explicate "otherness" could also be supportive to a link with Yoder. At first glance, Levinas' use of phenomenology appears to indicate the necessity of a philosophical grid for developing and explaining otherness. This link between otherness and phenomenology appears to counter the idea that one can tie otherness back to a particular or traditional claim. Levinas, who is primarily known for his work as a philosopher, was also quite interested in his Jewish heritage. His interest in Judaism is important because he was also able to make an argument for otherness through its resources. Levinas' writings on Judaism and his

---

8. Yoder, *Christian Witness to the State*. I also give a brief account of this argument in the introduction.

9. Yoder, *Body Politics*.

use of the Hebrew scriptures throughout his philosophical writing give evidence to the fact that otherness is not solely limited to a phenomenological investigation.[10] The import of this recognition is that otherness is not conditioned by phenomenology; it is not produced by phenomenology. Otherness exists with or without phenomenology, but phenomenology is a helpful way for Levinas to articulate the importance of otherness in terms that his interlocutors will understand.

Coming at this from a different angle one could view Levinas' use of phenomenology as a way to point back to Judaism. Drawing from Edith Wyschogrod's description of Steven Kepnes understanding of postmodern philosophy,[11] one is able to view how philosophy becomes a tool for rediscovering the Jewish tradition. The danger of modernity, according to Wyschogrod, is that it seeks to eliminate the particularity of the Jewish tradition for the sake of the universal. Kepnes views postmodern Jewish philosophy as a way to "return to Judaism."[12] Philosophy is a tool, in Kepnes's view, that enables Jewish philosophers to rediscover the particular importance of Judaism. Jewish thinkers no longer have to sacrifice their religious commitments because they want to work in philosophy; postmodern thought enables them to have both. Levinas' use of phenomenology seems to fit into a similar vein. Although he made special efforts to divorce philosophy from theology in his writings, one can still detect numerous places where the two coincide. Levinas' phenomenological description of otherness is for the dismantling of the primacy of the philosophical tradition. Levinas' desire to put philosophy into its proper place may coincide with Steven Kepnes's criticism of modernist approaches to Jewish Philosophy.[13] Kepnes argues that the modernist approach leads to a "turning away from Judaism." In order to do philosophical work in that vein one must repress one's particularity; one must forsake the particular for the universal. Levinas' phenomenology of otherness dismantles this necessity by reinserting the primacy of the particular over against the universal. Levinas' views

---

10. Emmanuel Levinas often utilizes scriptural accounts throughout his writings, both philosophical and religious, to aide in articulating his concerns regarding otherness. See also his *Difficult Freedom*.

11. Wyschogrod, "Trends in Postmodern Jewish Philosophy: Contexts of a Conversation" in Kepnes, Ochs, and Gibbs, *Reasoning After Revelation: Dialogues in Postmodern Jewish Philosophy*, 123–36.

12. Ibid., 125.

13. Kepnes, "Postmodern Jewish Thinking," in Kepnes, Ochs, and Gibbs, *Reasoning After Revelation: Dialogues in Postmodern Jewish Philosophy*, 24–27.

on otherness exposes the false idolatry of Western philosophy and thereby opens a way to return to Judaism. Philosophy does not replace the particular claims of the tradition but now serves to keep them in focus.

Looking at the issue from this angle we can see that Levinas is not looking to do away with his religious heritage, but may be seeking to translate its insights to the wider world. This effort to translate is akin to Yoder's invitation to translate Christian claims. Just as John's gospel utilizes the "logos" mythology to spread Christian claims so also might Levinas be using phenomenology to help awaken people to the reality of otherness. John's gospel does not allow the "logos" material to set the agenda; instead it puts it into service for its own purposes. Levinas' use of phenomenology can be interpreted as paralleling this maneuver. Levinas is not interested in reasserting the priority of philosophy over all forms of knowledge; instead, he is trying to dethrone it so that the particular other person is no longer swallowed up by its thematization. Phenomenology is a tool to accomplish this goal because it works to let otherness appear—it gives otherness the first word in the argument.

Certainly a more thorough inspection would need to be made in order to buttress the claims being made here, but it is clear that Levinas' use of phenomenology is not meant to reestablish the primacy of philosophy so that all other discourses would need to bow to its mastery.[14] The idea that Levinas sought to transform his religious heritage into purely philosophical categories misses his continuing work in Jewish thought and practice as well as his insistence to make space for the particularity of the other person. This coincides well with Yoder's concerns regarding philosophical work. Yoder's worry is that Christians have too often transformed their claims into philosophical categories in order to prove their perspective, but only at the cost of losing the particularity of their tradition. Yoder did not see a philosophy that could serve to translate and articulate Christian claims without compromising the identity of its origins, but Levinas' use of phenomenology is not meant to lose sight of the particular; it is meant to buttress the particular in the face of the universal. Yoder's worries are abated because Levinas shows a way to use philosophy that does not compromise the particular.

---

14. Levinas, "God and Philosophy" in *Emmanuel Levinas*, 129–48.

Question Two

The second issue correlates with the difference of opinion between Levinas and Yoder with regard to violence. Levinas' monumental study *Totality and Infinity*[15] began with a description of the violent nature of the politics of being. This discussion of war and violence set the tone for the rest of his study and it helped to fuel Jacques Derrida's labeling of Levinas as a pacifist.[16] Levinas resisted this label throughout his life by trying to show that his work sought to overcome a certain type of violence, which opposed itself to morality, rather than trying to overcome violence in general. The violence he had in mind was "the art of foreseeing war and of winning it by every means—politics—is henceforth enjoined as the very exercise of reason."[17] This type of violence failed to take account of the human toll it exacted. The "win at all costs" mentality continued the political struggle to persevere in being. Levinas' criticism of this violence was aimed at its complicity with the ontological destruction of otherness rather than the act of violence itself. Levinas believed that violence might be needed to help secure one's responsibility to the other person, especially with the advent of the third party.[18] The only kind of violence that Levinas seems to want to exclude is those forms of violence that begin outside of the recognition of one's responsibility to the other.

---

15. Levinas, *Totality and Infinity*.

16. Derrida, "Violence and Metaphysics: An Essay on the Thought of Emmanuel Levinas" in *Writing and Difference*, 79–153. Derrida's offers two locations for this pacifist label in his brief three point summary of Levinas' work (83): "A thought, finally, which liberates itself from a philosophy fascinated by the 'visage of being that shows itself in war'" and "This thought calls upon the ethical relationship—a *nonviolent* relationship to the infinite as infinitely other, to the Other...(italics mine)" One of the major themes of Derrida's work is to show how violence continues to linger in Levinas' project; the very language that Levinas must use implicates his work in the very violence he seeks to overcome. Levinas takes on this argument in his *Otherwise than Being*.

17. Levinas, *Totality and Infinity*, 21.

18. The ending sections of *Otherwise Than Being* contain this argument. Levinas, *Otherwise Than Being*, 131–72 (153–62). Levinas links the use of force with the necessity of utilizing ontological thought after one comes to realize the new starting point of the other. See his interview "Violence of the Face" in *Alterity and Transcendence*, 171–72. Also, Levinas was criticized (Caygill, *Levinas and the Political*) for his reaction to the events of 1982 between Lebanon and Israel where he was reticent to condemn the massacres at the Sabra and Chatila camps in Israeli occupied Lebanon (1). The interview that Caygill references is transcribed and translated (by Jonathan Romney) in Seán Hand's *Levinas Reader*, 289–97.

The Trace of the Face in the Politics of Jesus

The fact that Levinas saw violence in defense of another as possibly legitimate does not easily sit with Yoder's commitment to pacifism. The end result of a comparative exercise between these two figures must include a more thorough discussion of their differences regarding the use or non-use of violence. Two problems arise from this interaction. First, one may be led to misconstrue Levinas as supporting a purely pacifist position or second, one may be reifying the portrait of Yoder's pacifism as "utopian" and "unrealistic" because he does not seem to have a distinctive description of violence. The end result is that otherness for Levinas does not necessarily preclude violence while for Yoder it does.

Possible responses to this issue can come from at least two different angles. First, although Levinas does not consider himself a pacifist it has not stopped some of his students from pushing his work into that direction. Roger Burggraeve's *The Wisdom of Love in the Service of Love*[19] utilizes Levinas' materials to support a commitment to pacifism. Burggraeve argues through Levinas' conception of otherness for the viability of a pacifist response to issues of justice and war. By starting from the responsibility to the other, Burggraeve believes that alternative approaches to conflict can and do emerge. Drawing from Levinas' criticism of the ego, Burggraeve argues that political work, even positive political work, is doomed to fail because it is founded on an egocentric basis. This egocentric starting point results in a continuing use of violence to secure the ego from harm. Even principles and laws of justice, if generated from this egocentric perspective, carry within them the use of force. This force, as was described in Levinas' criticism of Western philosophy, does not always have to be physical—the thematization of the other is also a form of violence. Burggraeve argues that Levinas opens the door to political models based on dialogue and negotiation. The recognition of the other person in his/her otherness enables the conversation to proceed without the need to secure the ego. This alternative approach is pacifist because one is able to bring about change or end a conflict without the use of weapons. Burggraeve's argument does not gloss over the fact that Levinas still viewed violent response as possible,[20] but he seeks to show that Levinas' conception of otherness paves the way for creating

---

19. Burggraeve, *Wisdom of Love in the Service of Love*.

20. Ibid., 158–61. It should be noted that Burggraeve's ideas about pacifism are more akin to the U.S. Bishops Letter. The similarity is that pacifism is viewed as a real viable and preferred option, but the necessity of resorting to force, however small a possibility, continues to exist. See U.S. Catholic Bishops, "The Challenge of Peace: God's Promise and Our Response" in *Catholic Social Thought*, 489–571.

Conclusion

fresh nonviolent approaches to socio-political issues and concerns. Burggraeve argues that the initial starting point of a Levinasian politics carves out space for thinking nonviolently about these concerns. The idea of otherness invites the employment of alternative ways of dealing with those issues. Burggraeve's work, then, stands as an invitation to push Levinas' work in the direction of pacifism. Levinas' search for a radically different starting point for politics enables thinkers to try and develop a more pacifist approach. Burggraeve's work is only one move in this direction, but it does signal the possibility of more work in this area.

The second angle of response deals with Yoder's nuanced account of pacifism and violence. Too often many readers of Yoder fall into the trap of describing pacifism and violence in simplistic terms. Pacifism is associated with the complete rejection of violence while violence is often defined as an unbridled lust for destruction. Yoder did not reduce violence and pacifism to these two positions. He recognized the multiplicity of ways that violence and pacifism were enacted. *Nevertheless*[21] is one place where Yoder takes care to delineate no less than twenty types of pacifism. These nuanced accounts of pacifism help to clarify the debates surrounding pacifism and violence. One of the more interesting features of this book is Yoder's insistence to include Just War thinking as a form of pacifism. According to Yoder, the features of this position move in the direction of pacifism because it does not fall prey to the traps of total war. The effort to look closely at the use of war and to draw important limiting principles to guide its implementation are on the trajectory, albeit at its most initial moments, toward the limitation and cessation of hostilities. The recognition of this position, which continues to view violence as acceptable in certain cases, as a form of pacifism indicates that the interaction between Levinas and Yoder is viable. Yoder's ability to detect a "pacifist impulse"[22] within Just War reasoning enables him to converse with Just War thinkers. A conversation can be constructed even with Levinas' insistence that violence might still occur

21. Yoder, *Nevertheless*. Interestingly, Burggraeve's pacifism would fall under something like Just War thinking because he continues to rely on instrumentality for evaluating the rightness and wrongness of the use of force. Burggraeve's recognition that some violence may still be necessary indicates that pacifism is acceptable until it is no longer effective. Yoder's view on pacifism will be different at this point because for him being pacifist is not related to its effectiveness. This does not mean that Yoder does not think that pacifism can accomplish political goals, but that Christians are pacifists regardless of whether they accomplish them.

22. I have borrowed this term from Harvey L. Dyck's book dedicated to Peter Brock, *Pacifist Impulse in Historical Perspective*.

because Yoder recognized that not all uses of violence are the same. Just because Levinas did not adhere to a full blown pacifist position does not mean that Yoder would be reticent to talk with him about otherness and its possibilities for socio-political issues. In fact, Yoder would seek to learn from Levinas even though he and Levinas do not at first agree.

Question Three

The third and final issue deals with the feminist criticisms that have been leveled at both thinkers. Levinas' construal of otherness, especially as it is mapped out in terms of gender, and Yoder's articulation of revolutionary subordination incorporate elements that appear to restore modes of thinking that are pointed toward oppressing women. Both thinkers argue for their position in terms that identify and limit the roles of women;[23] i.e. the role and shape of a woman's life is predetermined by mandates that call for certain types of suffering service, which are necessary for upholding the moral order. Levinas conceives of otherness in terms of radical substitution while Yoder maintains that the proper Christian response to unjust orders is subordination. Levinas and Yoder demonstrate a lack of respect for the work of feminists who have identified and described how these calls for suffering service are imposed on women. Drawing from the works of Rosemary Radford Ruether[24] and Barbara Andolsen,[25] the ethical call for self-denial has historically been attached to the feminine gender. Suffering service, which is characterized by a radical reduction of the self's interests for the sake of the other, is a danger for women because it has been their plight to bear this service. The work of Joanne Carlson Brown and Carole R. Bohn has furthered this argument by noting that this attachment of suffering onto women may be inherently connected to Christian doctrine. The very idea of suffering service, which is posited most clearly in Christian theories of atonement, is the flaw.[26] One of the main features of this

---

23. Levinas' description of the feminine as "absolutely other" and his use of the role of a woman in an erotic relationship are just two examples of this issue. See his *Time and the Other*, 84–94.

24. I am relying chiefly on Ruether's chapter "Suffering and Redemption: The Cross and Atonement in Feminist Theology" found in her work *Introducing Redemption in Christian Feminism*, 95–107. For a radical set of critiques of the use of suffering to limit the experience of women see this collection of essays *Christianity, Patriarchy, and Abuse*.

25. Andolsen, "Agape in Feminist Ethics," 69–81.

26. Brown and Bohn, eds., *Christianity, Patriarchy, and Abuse*.

argument is that Christian ideas about atonement have planted a seed of acceptance in the minds of women; it is their duty to accept suffering and by doing so they exemplify the Christian conception of redemption.

The idea of self-denial, which is integral for Levinas and Yoder, is viewed as being oppressive to women because it has historically been attached to the feminine gender. It has been up to women to bear the burden of demonstrating the ethical necessity of sacrificing oneself for the other. Brown and Bohn demonstrate that this necessity to attach self-denial to women could be an inherent flaw within the tradition itself thereby strengthening the interconnection between suffering service and the oppression of women. The centrality of the subordination of the self in Levinas and Yoder means that one must work toward mounting a response in order to maintain the importance of their work.

Attempting to generate a response through Levinas' materials is one way that can help to alleviate some of the problems listed above while also erasing some of the problems associated with Yoder's conception. In order to get at this response, it is imperative we explicate more clearly some of the feminist concerns surrounding Levinas' conception of otherness.[27] There have been two fundamental critiques leveled by feminists. The first way incorporates the critique of suffering service. The conception of "one-for-the-other" places an infinite responsibility to care for the other and this care results in a radical life of self-denial. The problems of agape love resurface in the Levinas' conception of the subject. One is capable of claiming that Levinas' conception of the ego, especially when Levinas utilizes terms like "substitution" or "hostage" to describe it, reinstitutes a suffering that is characterized as a total denial of the self.

Leora Batnitzky's article "Encountering the Modern Subject in Levinas"[28] combined with Levinas' material on the advent of the third party helps to alleviate some of the pressure from this perspective. Batnitzky argues that Levinas does not argue for a complete destruction of subjectivity; certainly, he argues that subjectivity is made possible in its encounter with the other, but it retains a "separate" sense of self.[29] Batnitzky's argument is that Levinas' work is not an attempt to completely do away with subjectivity,

---

27. Historically Simone de Beauvoir and Luce Irigaray have been looked to for initiating a critique of Levinas' work. See Simone de Beauvoir, *Second Sex*, and Luce Irigaray, "The Fecundity of the Caress: A Reading of Levinas, *Totality and Infinity*, 'Phenomenology of Eros,'" in *Feminist Interpretations of Emmanuel Levinas*, 119–44.

28. Batnitzky, "Encountering the Modern Subject in Levinas," 6–21.

29. Ibid., 17.

but to reframe it in terms of its dynamic with the other. The presence of a separable self is given a practical moment in Levinas' mention of the third party. The encounter of the one to the other is only the beginning of the self's journey. Because it is a beginning there is yet a further moment when calculations and reserves can be put into action. In other words, Levinas' description about the self taken hostage by the encounter with the other is only a tracing out of where to begin.

The second angle of the feminist critique of Levinas derives from Simone de Beauvoir's comments regarding Levinas' use of feminine imagery in *Time and the Other*.[30] Beauvoir argued that Levinas continued to postulate that women were only part of the male experience of growth and transcendence. The way that Levinas describes the work of women in explicating otherness leaves no room for their own self-development. According to Tina Chanter, Beauvoir's critical remarks pointed out the way in which Levinas appeared to maintain a connection with the "long line of male thinkers who have subordinated women to men, refused to construe the relation between the sexes as reciprocal, denied women full subjectivity, and consigned them to the rank of the inessential."[31] Although Chanter goes on to show that Beauvoir's comments fail to recognize some of the deeper goals of Levinas' project, she is still correct to assert that women are defined by characteristics stereotypically associated with the female gender[32] and that their experience is solely defined through the male gender.

These criticisms are not easily explained away. For instance, Chanter remarks how for Levinas the feminine plays an important role as other in breaking apart the hegemonic tyranny of Western philosophical thought. Levinas' characterization, then, appears to elevate the feminine gender by utilizing it as the locus for this breakthrough. It would seem that Levinas has helped to champion feminist concerns, but a closer inspection finds that this characterization of the feminine gender continues to force a woman's experience through the lens of a male-dominated perspective. Drawing from the work of Luce Irigaray, Chanter describes how this prioritization continues to place women in the role of facilitating a man's experience of transcendence.[33] Levinas' use of sexualized imagery to help make his case compounds the issue. His characterization of the woman's role in

30. de Beauvoir, *Second Sex*; Emmanuel Levinas, *Time and the Other*.
31. Chanter, "Introduction" in *Feminist Interpretations of Emmanuel Levinas*, 2.
32. Some of these characterizations are mysterious, other, weak, and homemaker.
33. Ibid., 3.

demonstrating the reality of transcendence continues the male hegemonic modes of domination. This is most problematic in Levinas' description of the woman as establishing and supporting the home.[34] The idea that women are to play "homemaker" in order to help facilitate transcendence restates the fact that a woman continues to be only an implement for the experience of men.

Chanter's volume is an attempt to see if there is a way beyond these issues. One of the contributors, Claire Katz,[35] lays out a plan for overcoming these problems. She acknowledges the substantive components of both Beauvoir and Irigaray's critiques. In fact, she believes that, at face value, Levinas' use of femininity in *Time and the Other* and *Totality and Infinity* endanger his whole project. Two aspects stand out in their critique: the characterization of women as homemaker and as child bearer. In both cases Levinas describes women, whether real or metaphorically, as implements for male transcendence. In both cases women are excluded from participating in the ethical and are forced to serve as facilitators, whether by making the home more habitable or by bearing a son. Women are certainly constitutive of the possibility of the ethical order, but they are merely its constructors; they cannot participate in it. Katz turns to the example of Ruth as providing the impetus for moving beyond this impasse.

Katz argues, in contrast to Irigaray, that habitation and erotic fecundity contain excesses that enable the Levinas interpreter to push past the feminine limitations. Katz's point is that Levinas' description of transcendence does not have to be limited to the contours of his argument. She believes that one can utilize the framework of his conception without having to be locked into its gender driven elements. In other words, although Levinas reinforces his argument through gendered stereotypes, the argument continues to be effective even after one disarms these elements. Katz is not arguing that there aren't issues with Levinas, but she does believe that a closer inspection will reveal that the argument stands without these impediments. The idea of fecundity, which is characterized by the birth of the son as the culmination of the erotic relationship, appears to make women only into facilitators of this masculine transcendence. This idea of fecundity, however, exceeds this limitation because the birth of the son is

---

34. The clearest example of this is Levinas' chapter on dwelling in *Totality and Infinity*, 152–74.

35. Katz, "Reinhabiting the House of Ruth: Exceeding the Limits of the Feminine in Levinas" in *Feminist Interpretations of Emmanuel Levinas*, 145–70; Katz, *Levinas, Judaism, and the Feminine*.

further linked to the importance of instituting a future and spreading the image of God. According to Katz, "it is possible to broaden this conception of 'birth' and 'child'...we have a responsibility nonetheless to make every attempt to respond in accordance with the ethical *mitzvot* of the Torah."[36] Drawing from Levinas' Jewish background, Katz is able to show that the sexual relationship is broader than the birthing of children. Sexuality is also a part of the process of "repairing" the world.[37] This act of mending the world serves to indicate that there is more to transcendence than the stereotypical gender traits.

Habitation, in a similar fashion, also exceeds its original description.[38] Katz points to the example of Ruth for demonstrating this point. Habitation, in *Totality and Infinity*, is the return movement back to the same. This is a necessary part of Levinasian subjectivity and the feminine plays her role in establishing this home: it is hospitality. Hospitality, however, is not limited to the maintenance of the home for this returning movement. Katz argues that Ruth's actions toward Naomi demonstrate both the hospitality of habitation and its greater ethical significance. The example of Ruth broadens Levinas' conception of feminine hospitality by integrating itself into the ethical. For Katz, this example shows a weakness in Levinas' thought because he does not consider relationships between two persons of the same sex, but the biblical example of Ruth aids the extension of Levinas' own findings to such relational dynamics. Ruth fulfills her "feminine" role, but in so doing she moves past the point of merely providing a home. Ruth is not only providing a hospitable area for Naomi, but she is also manifesting the ethical order without the presence of a male figure. Katz wants to show that even though Levinas does not entertain this reading it is not contrary to his work to see Ruth in this light. Ruth exceeds Levinas' understanding of habitation but does not eradicate its importance; she remains well within the confines of the Levinasian framework.

Katz's work demonstrates that one can begin to move past the gendered materials of Levinas' work without completely abandoning his original aims. She is able to construct her findings in such a way that both accepts the feminist criticisms of his work and continues to build off his insights. According to Katz, Ruth is the consummate example of feminine

---

36. Katz, *Levinas, Judaism, and the Feminine*, 87.

37. Ibid., 87.

38. Katz, "Reinhabiting the House of Ruth: Exceeding the Limits of the Feminine in Levinas" in *Feminist Interpretations of Emmanuel Levinas*, 145–70.

hospitality. This characterization will continue to receive criticism for maintaining the position that women are to fulfill the requirements of their femininity in certain ways. Nevertheless, Katz is able to show that in and through this feminine modality Ruth exceeds the expectations of her role—she constitutes the ethical through her hospitality. In other words, she participates in the ethical without having to rely on a masculine presence: Ruth experiences the transcendent ethical order. There is, I think, a way to use this line of reasoning to help alleviate some of the critical issues regarding Yoder's conception of revolutionary subordination. Yoder argued that this practice could bring about change to the social order, but many are hard pressed to see how this change can come about. The idea that one is to subordinate oneself to the governing structures of one's existence, even if they are oppressive, seems very unlikely to lead to any lasting change. Katz's description of Ruth, however, provides a possible sample of such change taking place. Katz's claim that something more is going on in Ruth's situation than the mere upholding of gendered roles becomes a possible avenue for exemplifying Yoder's belief that change can occur through subordination. Although the changes are subtle, one could begin to try and mount an argument that would demonstrate how this practice could bring about change.

These three issues, as noted above, demand a more thorough accounting. They are questions that would need to be addressed if further work might be done through a comparison between Yoder and Levinas. This brief interlude has not sought to exhaustively solve these issues, but looked to point out some possible responses. The experimental effort to extract insights from Levinas' conception of otherness for extending Yoder's legacy will have to address these issues, but it also promises to provide more avenues of dialogue for Christian theological and moral discourses.

Final Thoughts

The original goal of this project was to experimentally link Yoder with a portion of the Western philosophical tradition in order to help further his legacy. Certainly his *Politics* will continue to be read, but only in terms of its argument for pacifism. Pacifism, like revolutionary subordination, is merely the outgrowth of Jesus' political vision. What is missed by many is that pacifism is a secondary story for Yoder. The larger vision of Jesus' political vision is reduced to the practice of pacifism and this only limits

Yoder's future impact on Christian thinking. Levinas' philosophical work, however, helps to reorient Yoder's readers to see this larger narrative at work. It provides a "middle axiom" for translating his insights for engaging the wider society. As one of the titles of Yoder's work indicates, Christians are to be *For the Nations*. The Christian tradition is a witnessing community. It cannot avoid the wider world for to do so is to be unfaithful. This engagement, however, cannot be fully predicated on the particulars of the Christian tradition but must also be aided by efforts to find a middle ground for constructing a dialogue. Nevertheless, learning to translate itself without losing its identity is a part of that engagement. Levinas' conception of otherness provides the ability to handle this two-sided issue: Christians can communicate their convictions in terms that the wider world is more likely to understand while also maintaining its commitment to be faithful witnesses to the politics of Jesus.

> Our choice is after all, he tells us, the same as the one Jesus faced, the one Eve faced. Will we reach out for dignity, importance, achievement, for godlikeness as a thing to grasp and to hold? Will we grab for sovereignty in the small world we can control? Or might we learn to trust that our worthiness as bearers of God's image was given to us, so that we need not grab it? Given us, in fact, to be passed on, to be given further?[39]

Yoder's call for Christians to be mindful of how they engage the world is a call to responsibility for the other, even the enemy other. Rather than trying to mold and shape the world into a monolithic model, Yoder calls Christians to be the kind of people who practice a politics of inclusion and dialogue. Yoder's comment here states that God's image is something "to be passed on," something "to be given further." The politics of otherness is an alternative way of living in the world, a way that subordinates the self and its desires so that one approaches another in the spirit of service, attending to his/her vulnerability. In this manner, new possibilities and new politics can be discovered; a revolution can occur.

---

39. Yoder, *He Came Preaching Peace*, 94.

Bibliography

Anderson, Stephen D. "*The Politics of Jesus.*" *Trinity Journal* 3 (1974) 77–79.
Andolsen, Barbara Hilkert. "Agape in Feminist Ethics." *Journal of Religious Ethics* 9 (1981) 69–81.
Armour, Ellen T. *Deconstruction, Feminist Theology, and the Problem of Difference: Subverting the Race/Gender Divide*. Chicago: The University of Chicago Press, 1999.
Atterton, Peter. "Levinas and the Language of Peace: A Response to Derrida." *Philosophy Today* 36 (1992) 59–70.
Baird, Marie L. "Revisioning Christian Theology in Light of Emmanuel Levinas' Ethics of Responsibility." *Journal of Ecumenical Studies* 36 (1999) 340–51.
Barber, Daniel. "The Particularity of Jesus and the Time of the Kingdom: Philosophy and Theology in Yoder." *Modern Theology* 23 (2007) 63–89.
Batnitzky, Leora. "Encountering the Modern Subject in Levinas." *Yale French Studies* 104 (2003) 6–21.
Bauman, Whitney. "Essentialism, Universalism, and Violence: Unpacking the Ideology of Patriarchy." *The Journal of Women and Religion* 19/20 (2003) 52–71.
Bauman, Zygmunt. *Postmodern Ethics*. Oxford: Blackwell, 1993.
Bender, Harold S. "The Anabaptist Vision." *Church History* 13 (1944) 3–24.
Bergo, Bettina. "Ontology, Transcendence, and Immanence in Emmanuel Levinas' Philosophy." *Research In Phenomenology* 35 (2005) 141–77.
Berkhof, Hendrik. *Christ and the Powers*. Translated by John Howard Yoder. Scottdale, PA: Herald, 1977.
Bernasconi, Robert, and Simon Critchley, editors. *Re-Reading Levinas*. Bloomington: Indiana University Press, 1991.
Bloechl, Jeffrey, editor. *The Face of the Other & The Trace of God: Essays on the Philosophy of Emmanuel Levinas*. New York: Fordham University Press, 2000.
Blum, Roland Paul. "Emmanuel Levinas' Theory of Commitment." *Philosophy and Phenomenological Research* 44 (1983) 145–68.
Boyarin, Daniel. "Judaism as a Free Church: Footnotes to John Howard Yoder's The Jewish-Christian Schism Revisited." *Cross Currents* 56 (2007) 6–21.
Brock, Peter. *Varieties of Pacifism: A Survey from Antiquity to the Outset of the Twentieth Century*. 4th ed. Syracuse, NY: Syracuse University Press, 1998.
Brown, Joanne Carlson, and Carole R. Bohn, editors. *Christianity, Patriarchy, and Abuse: A Feminist Critique*. Cleveland: Pilgrim, 1989.

Bibliography

Burggraeve, Roger. *The Wisdom of Love in the Service of Love: Emmanuel Levinas on Justice, Peace, and Human Rights*. Milwaukee: Marquette University Press, 2002.

Burggraeve, Roger, and Marc Vervenne, editors. *Swords Into Plowshares: Theological Reflections on Peace*. Louvain: Peeters, 1991.

Burrell, David, and Stanley Hauerwas. "From System to Story: An Alternative Pattern for Rationality in Ethics." In *Knowledge, Value, and Belief*, edited by H. Tristam Engelhardt, Jr. and Daniel Callahan, 111–52. New York: The Hastings Center, 1977.

Carter, Craig A. *The Politics of the Cross: The Theology and Social Ethics of John Howard Yoder*. Grand Rapids: Brazos, 2001.

———. "Beyond Theocracy and Individualism: The Significance of John Howard Yoder's Ecclesiology for Evangelicalism." In *The Community of the Word: Toward an Evangelical Ecclesiology*, edited by William J. Abraham, Ellen T. Charry and John Webster, 173–87. Downers Grove, IL: InterVarsity, 2005.

Castelo, Daniel. "A Yoderian Appraisal of Latin American Liberation Theology." *The Asbury Theological Journal* 57/58 (2002/2003) 25–40.

Caygill, Howard. *Levinas & the Political*. London: Routledge, 2002.

Chanter, Tina, editor. *Feminist Interpretations of Emmanuel Levinas*. University Park: The Pennsylvania State University Press, 2001.

Childress, James F. "Reinhold Niebuhr's Critique of Pacifism." *The Review of Politics* 36 (1974) 467–91.

Clark, Jack L. "*The Politics of Jesus*." *Lutheran Quarterly* 25 (1973) 421–22.

Clifford, Anne M. *Introducing Feminist Theology*. Maryknoll, NY: Orbis, 2001.

Coles, Romand. *Beyond Gated Politics: Reflections for the Possibility of Democracy*. Minneapolis: University of Minnesota Press, 2005.

———. *Self/Power/Other: Political Theory and Dialogical Ethics*. Ithaca, NY: Cornell University Press, 1992.

———. "The Wild Patience of John Howard Yoder: 'Outsiders' and the 'Otherness of the Church.'" *Modern Theology* 18 (2002) 305–31.

Conover, Pamela Johnston, and Virginia Sapiro. "Gender, Feminist Consciousness, and War." *American Journal of Political Science* 37 (1993) 1079–99.

Critchley, Simon. *The Ethics of Deconstruction: Derrida and Levinas*. 2nd ed. Edinburgh: Edinburgh University Press, 1999.

Critchley, Simon, and Robert Bernasconi, editors. *The Cambridge Companion to Levinas*. Cambridge: Cambridge University Press, 2002.

Cullmann, Oscar. *The Early Church*. London: SCM, 1956

Davenport, John J. "Levinas's Agapeistic Metaphysics of Morals: Absolute Passivity and the Other as Eschatological Hierophany." *Journal of Religious Ethics* 26 (Fall 1998): 331–66.

Davis, Colin. *Levinas: An Introduction*. Notre Dame, IN: The University of Notre Dame Press, 1996.

Deats, Paul. "Protestant Social Ethics and Pacifism." In *War or Peace?: The Search for New Answers*, edited by Thomas A. Shannon. Maryknoll, NY: Orbis, 1980.

DeFerrari, Teresa M. "John H. Yoder, *The Politics of Jesus*." *The Catholic Biblical Quarterly* 36 (1974) 149–50.

Derrida, Jacques. *Adieu To Emmanuel Levinas*. Translated by Pascale-Anne Brault and Michael Naas. Stanford, CA: Stanford University Press, 1999.

———. *Writing and Difference*. Translated by Alan Bass. Chicago: The University of Chicago Press, 1978.

Donahue, John R. "The Politics of Jesus." *Theological Studies* 35 (1974) 179–80.

Drazenovich, George. "Towards a Levinasian Understanding of Christian Ethics: Emmanuel Levinas and the Phenomenology of the Other." *Cross Currents* 54 (2005) 37–54.

Dudiak, Jeffrey. *Structures of Violence, Structures of Peace: Levinasian Reflections on Just War and Pacifism.*" In *Knowing Other-wise: Philosophy at the Threshold of Spirituality.* Edited by James H. Olthius, 159–71. New York: Fordham University Press, 1997.

Dudiak, Jeffrey. *The Intrigue of Ethics: A Reading of the Idea of Discourse in the Thought of Emmanuel Levinas.* New York: Fordham University Press, 2001.

Dyck, Cornelius J. *An Introduction to Mennonite History.* Scottdale, PA: Herald, 1993.

Edwards, George R. "The Politics of Jesus: Vicit Agnus Noster." *The Mennonite Quarterly Review* 48 (1974) 534–38.

Elshtain, Jean Bethke. "Ethics in the Women's Movement." *Annals of the American Academy of Political and Social Science* 515 (1991) 126–39.

———. "Reflections on War and Political Discourse: Realism, Just War, and Feminism in a Nuclear Age." *Political Theory* 13 (1985) 39–57.

Fiorenza, Elisabeth Schüssler. *Bread Not Stone: The Challenge of Feminist Biblical Interpretation.* Boston: Beacon, 1995.

———. *In Memory of Her: A Feminist Theological Reconstruction of Christian Origins.* New York: Crossroad, 1992.

———. *Wisdom Ways: Introducing Feminist Biblical Interpretation.* Maryknoll, NY: Orbis, 2001.

Flanders, H. J., Jr. "The Politics of Jesus: Vicit Agnus Noster." *Journal of Church and State* 18 (1976) 115–17.

Flescher, Andrew. "Love and Justice in Reinhold Niebuhr's Prophetic Christian Realism and Emmanuel Levinas' Ethics of Responsibility: Treading Between Pacifism and Just-War Theory." *The Journal of Religion* 80 (2000) 61–82.

Friesen, Duane K. "Toward a Theology of Culture: A Dialogue with John H. Yoder and Gordon Kaufman." *The Conrad Grebel Review* 16 (1998) 39–64.

Fulkerson, Mary McClintock. *Changing the Subject: Women's Discourses and Feminist Theology.* Minneapolis: Fortress, 1994.

Gibbs, Robert. *Correlations In Rosenzweig and Levinas.* Princeton, NJ: Princeton University Press, 1992.

Gingerich, Ray. "Theological Foundations for an Ethic of Nonviolence: Was Yoder's God a Warrior?." *The Mennonite Quarterly Review* 77 (2003) 417–35.

Grimsrud, Ted. "Pacifism and Knowing: 'Truth' in the Theological Ethics of John Howard Yoder." *The Mennonite Quarterly Review* 77 (2003) 403–15.

Gustafson, James M. *Ethics from a Theocentric Perspective.* 2 vols. Chicago: The University of Chicago Press, 1981/1984.

———. *Moral Discernment in the Christian Life: Essays in Theological Ethics.* Edited by Theo A. Boer and Paul E. Capetz. Louisville: Westminster John Knox, 2007.

———. *Protestant and Roman Catholic Ethics: Prospects for Rapprochement.* Chicago: The University of Chicago Press, 1978.

Harink, Douglas. "For or Against the Nations: Yoder and Hauerwas, What's the Difference?." *Toronto Journal Of Theology* 17 (2001) 167–85.

Hauerwas, Stanley. *After Christendom.* Nashville: Abingdon, 1991.

———. *Against the Nations: War and Survival in a Liberal Society.* Minneapolis: Winston, 1985.

Bibliography

———. *A Better Hope: Resources for a Church Confronting Capitalism, Democracy, and Postmodernity*. Grand Rapids: Brazos, 2000.

———. *Christian Existence Today: Essays on Church, World and Living in Between*. Durham, NC: Labyrinth, 1988.

———. "Democratic Time: Lessons Learned from Yoder and Wolin." *Cross Currents* 55 (2006) 534–52.

———. *Dispatches from the Front: Theological Engagements with the Secular*. Durham, NC: Duke University Press, 1994.

———. *The Hauerwas Reader*. Edited by John Berkman and Michael Cartwright. Durham, NC: Duke University Press, 2001.

———. *In Good Company: The Church as Polis*. Notre Dame, IN: University of Notre Dame Press, 1995.

———. *The Peaceable Kingdom: A Primer in Christian Ethics*. Notre Dame, IN: University of Notre Dame Press, 1983.

———. *Performing the Faith: Bonhoeffer and the Practice of Nonviolence*. Grand Rapids: Brazos, 2004.

———. *Unleashing the Scriptures: Freeing the Bible from Captivity to America*. Nashville: Abingdon, 1993.

———. "The Virtues of Alasdair MacIntyre." *First Things* 176 (2007) 35–40.

———. *Vision and Virtue*. Notre Dame, IN: University of Notre Dame Press, 1981.

———. *With the Grain of the Universe: The Church's Witness and Natural Theology*. Grand Rapids: Brazos, 2001.

Hauerwas, Stanley, Chris K. Huebner, Harry J. Huebner, and Mark Thiessen Nation, editors. *The Wisdom of the Cross: Essays in Honor of John Howard Yoder*. Grand Rapids: Eerdmans, 1999.

Hauerwas, Stanley, and Romand Coles. *Christianity, Democracy, and the Radical Ordinary: Conversations Between a Radical Democrat and a Christian*. Theopolitical Visions 1. Eugene, OR: Cascade, 2008.

Hauerwas, Stanley, and William H. Willimon. *Resident Aliens*. Nashville: Abingdon, 1989.

———. *Where Resident Aliens Live*. Nashville: Abingdon, 1996.

Horowitz, Asher, and Gad Horowitz, editors. *Difficult Justice: Commentaries on Levinas and Politics*. Toronto: University of Toronto Press, 2006.

Horton, John, and Susan Mendus, editors. *After MacIntyre: Critical Perspectives on the Work of Alasdair MacIntyre*. Notre Dame, IN: University of Notre Dame Press, 1994.

Huebner, Chris K. "Mennonites and Narrative Theology: The Case of John Howard Yoder." *The Conrad Grebel Review* 16 (1998) 15–38.

———. *A Precarious Peace: Yoderian Explorations on Theology, Knowledge, and Identity*. Scottdale, PA: Herald, 2006.

Hutchens, B. C. *Levinas: A Guide for the Perplexed*. London: Continuum, 2004.

Job, John. "The Politics of Jesus." *The Evangelical Quarterly* 68 (1996) 371.

Johnson, James Turner. "Historical Tradition and Moral Judgment: The Case of Just War Tradition." *The Journal of Religion* 64 (1984) 299–317.

Jones, L. Gregory. "Alasdair MacIntyre on Narrative, Community, and the Moral Life." *Modern Theology* 4 (1987) 53–69.

Jones, Serene. *Feminist Theory and Christian Theology: Cartographies of Grace*. Minneapolis: Fortress, 2000.

Kallenberg, Brad. "The Gospel Truth of Relativism." *The Scottish Journal of Theology* 53 (2000) 177–211.

Kates, Judith A., and Gail Twersky Reimer, editors. *Reading Ruth: Contemporary Women Reclaim a Sacred Story.* New York: Ballantine, 1994.

Katz, Claire Elise. *Levinas, Judaism, and the Feminine: The Silent Footsteps of Rebecca.* Bloomington, IN: Indiana University Press, 2003.

Kavka, Martin. "Saying Kaddish for Gillian Rose, or on Levinas and *Geltungsphilosophie*." In *Secular Theology: American Radical Theological Thought.* Edited by Clayton Crockett, 104-129. New York: Routledge, 2001.

Kepnes, Steven, Peter Ochs, and Robert Gibbs. *Reasoning After Religion: Dialogues in Jewish Philosophy.* Boulder, CO: Westview, 1998.

Klassen, Walter. "The Anabaptist Critique of Constantinian Christendom." *The Mennonite Quarterly Review* 55 (1981) 218-30.

———. "The Anabaptist Understanding of the Separation of the Church." *Church History* 46 (1977) 421-36.

Klassen, William. "John Howard Yoder and the Ecumenical Church." *The Conrad Grebel Review* 16 (1998) 77-81.

Kosky, Jeffrey L. "After the Death of God: Emmanuel Levinas and the Ethical Possibility of God." *Journal of Religious Ethics* 24 (1996) 235-59.

———. *Levinas and the Philosophy of Religion.* Bloomington: Indiana University Press, 2001.

Kroeker, P. Travis. "Is a Messianic Political Ethic Possible?: Recent Work by and about John Howard Yoder." *Journal of Religious Ethics* 33 (2005) 141-74.

———. "The War of the Lamb: Postmodernity and John Howard Yoder's Eschatological Genealogy of Morals." *The Mennonite Quarterly Review* 74 (2000) 295-310.

———. "Why O'Donovan's Christendom is not Constantinian and Yoder's Voluntariety is not Hobbesian: A Debate in Theological Politics Re-defined." *The Annual of the Society of Christian Ethics* 20 (2000) 41-64.

Kunz, George. *The Paradox of Power and Weakness: Levinas and an Alternative Paradigm for Pyschology.* Albany: State University of NewYork Press, 1998.

Lee, Jung H. "Neither Totality nor Infinity: Suffering the Other." *Journal of Religion* 79 (April 1999) 250-79.

Levinas, Emmanuel. *Alterity and Transcendence.* Translated by Michael B.

———. *Collected Philosophical Papers.* Translated by Alphonso Lingis. Pittsburgh: Duquesne University Press, 1998.

———. *Difficult Freedom: Essays on Judaism.* Translated by Sean Hand. Baltimore, MD: The Johns Hopkins University Press, 1997.

———. *Discovering Existence With Husserl.* Translated by Richard A. Cohen and Michael B. Smith. Evanston, IL: Northwestern University Press, 1998.

———. *Emmanuel Levinas: Basic Philosophical Writings.* Edited by Adriaan T. Peperzak, Simon Critchley, and Robert Bernasconi. Bloomington, IN: Indiana University Press, 1996.

———. *Entre Nous: On Thinking-of-the-Other.* Translated by Michael B. Smith and Barbara Harshav. New York: Columbia University Press, 1998.

———. *Ethics and Infinity: Conversations with Philippe Nemo.* Translated by Richard A. Cohen. Pittsburgh: Duquesne University Press, 2004.

———. *Existence & Existents.* Translated by Alphonso Lingis. Pittsburgh: Duquesne University Press, 2001.

———. *God, Death, and Time.* Translated by Bettina Bergo. Stanford, CA: Stanford University Press, 2000.

Bibliography

———. *In the Time of the Nations*. Translated by Michael B. Smith. London: Continuum, 2007.
———. *The Levinas Reader*. Edited by Sean Hand. Oxford: Blackwell, 1997.
———. *Of God Who Comes To Mind*. Translated by Bettina Bergo. Stanford, CA: Stanford University Press, 1998.
———. *On Escape*. Translated by Bettina Bergo. Stanford, CA: Stanford University Press, 2003.
———. *Otherwise Than Being: Or Beyond Essence*. Translated by Alphonso Lingis. Pittsburgh: Duquesne University Press, 2006.
———. *Outside the Subject*. Translated by Michael B. Smith. Stanford, CA: Stanford University Press, 1993.
———. *Proper Names*. Translated by Michael B. Smith. Stanford, CA: Stanford University Press, 1996.
———. *Time & the Other*. Translated by Richard A. Cohen. Pittsburgh: Duquesne University Press, 2002.
———. *Totality and Infinity: An Essay On Exteriority*. Translated by Alphonso Lingis. Pittsburgh: Duquesne University Press, 2002.
———. *Unforseen History*. Tranlsated by Nidra Poller. Chicago: University of Illinois Press, 2004.
Lindbeck, George A. *The Nature of Doctrine: Religion and Theology in a Postliberal Age*. Louisville: Westminster John Knox, 1984.
Littell, Franklin H. "Church and Sect." *Ecumenical Review* 6 (1954) 262–76.
Llewelyn, John. *Appositions of Jacques Derrida and Emmanuel Levinas*. Bloomington: Indiana University Press, 2002.
———. *Emmanuel Levinas: The Genealogy of Ethics*. London: Routledge, 1995.
MacIntyre, Alasdair. *After Virtue*. 2nd ed. Notre Dame, IN: University of Notre Dame Press, 1984.
———. *Dependent Rational Animals: Why Human Beings Need the Virtues*. Chicago: Open Court, 1999.
———. *Three Rival Versions of Moral Enquiry: Encyclopaedia, Genealogy, and Tradition*. Notre Dame, IN: University of Notre Dame Press, 1990.
———. *Whose Justice? Which Rationality?* Notre Dame, IN: University of Notre Dame Press, 1988.
Mack, Michael. "Franz Rosenzweig's and Emmanuel Levinas's Critique of German Idealism's Pseudotheology." *The Journal of Religion* 83 (2003) 56–78.
Martin, Francis. *The Feminist Question: Feminist Theology in the Light of Christian Tradition*. Grand Rapids: Eerdmans, 1994.
McAllister, Pam, editor. *Reweaving the Web of Life: Feminism and Nonviolence*. Philadelphia: New Society, 1982.
McCaughey, Martha. "The Fighting Spirit: Women's Self-Defense Training and the Discourse of Sexed Embodiment." *Gender and Society* 12 (1998) 277–300.
Meskin, Jacob. "Toward a New Understanding of the Work of Emmanuel Levinas." *Modern Judaism* 20 (2000) 78–102.
Milbank, John. "The Ethics of Self-Sacrifice." *First Things* 91 (1999) 33–38.
Miller, John W. "In the Footsteps of Marcion: Notes Toward an Understanding of John Howard Yoder's Theology." *The Conrad Grebel Review* 16 (1998) 82–92.
Moyn, Samuel. *Origins of the Other: Emmanuel Levinas Between Revelation and Ethics*. Ithaca, NY: Cornell University Press, 2005.

Murphy, Nancey, Brad J. Kallenberg, and Mark Thiessen Nation, editors. *Virtues and Practices in the Christian Tradition: Christian Ethics after MacIntyre*. Notre Dame, IN: University of Notre Dame Press, 2003.

Nation, Mark Thiessen. *John Howard Yoder: Mennonite Patience, Evangelical Witness, Catholic Convictions*. Grand Rapids: Eerdmans, 2006.

Neufeld, Justin. "Just War Theory, the Authorization of the State, and the Hermeneutics of Peoplehood: How John Howard Yoder can save Oliver O'Donovan from Himself." *International Journal of Systematic Theology* 8 (2006) 411–32.

Niebuhr, Reinhold. *Moral Man and Immoral Society*. New York, NY: Touchstone, 1995.

———. *The Nature and Destiny of Man*. 2 vols. Louisville: Westminster John Knox, 1996.

Niebuhr, H. Richard. *Christ and Culture*. New York: Harper Torchbooks, 1975.

———. *"The Responsibility of the Church for Society" and Other Essays by H. Richard Niebuhr*. Louisville: Westminster John Knox, 2008.

———. *The Responsible Self: An Essay in Christian Moral Philosophy*. Louisville: Westminster John Knox, 1999.

Ollenburger, Ben C., and Gayle Gerber Koontz, editors. *A Mind Patient and Untamed: Assessing John Howard Yoder's Contributions to Theology, Ethics, and Peacemaking*. Telford, PA: Cascadia, 2004.

Parsons, Susan Frank, editor. *The Cambridge Companion to Feminist Theology*. Cambridge: Cambridge University Press, 2002.

Peperzak, Adriaan Theodoor. *Beyond: The Philosophy of Emmanuel Levinas*. Evanston, IL: Northwestern University Press, 1999.

———. *To The Other: An Introduction to the Philosophy of Emmanuel Levinas*. West Lafayette, IN: Purdue University Press, 1993.

Pfeil, Margaret R. "John Howard Yoder's Pedagogical Approach: A Just War Tradition with Teeth and a Hermeneutic of Peace." *The Mennonite Quarterly Review* 76 (2002) 181–88.

Purcell, Michael. *Levinas and Theology*. Cambridge: Cambridge University Press, 2006.

Rasmussen, Larry, editor. *Reinhold Niebuhr: Theologian of Public Life*. London: Collins Liturgical, 1989.

Reimer, A. James. *Mennonites and Classical Theology: Dogmatic Foundations for Christian Ethics*. Kitchener: Pandora, 2001.

Robbins, Jill, editor. *Is It Righteous To Be?: Interviews with Emmanuel Levinas*. Stanford, CA: Stanford University Press, 2001.

Rose, Gillian. "Angry Angels – Simone Weil and Emmanuel Levinas." In *Judaism and Modernity*, 211–23. Oxford: Blackwell, 1993.

———. *Dialectic of Nihilism: Post-Structuralism and Law*. Oxford: Blackwell, 1984.

———. *The Broken Middle*. Oxford: Blackwell, 1992.

Rowland, Christopher. *The Cambridge Companion to Liberation Theology*. Cambridge: Cambridge University Press, 1999.

Ruether, Rosemary Radford. *Redemption in Christian Feminism*. Cleveland: Pilgrim, 2000.

———. *Sexism and God-Talk: Toward a Feminist Theology*. Boston, MA: Beacon, 1983.

———. "Feminism and Peace." *The Christian Century* 100 (1983) 771–76.

———. "Feminism, Future Hope, and the Crisis of Modernity." *Buddhist-Christian Studies* 18 (1998) 69–73.

———. "Redemptive Community in Christianity." *Buddhist-Christian Studies* 11 (1991) 217–30.

Bibliography

Searles, Patricia, and Ronald J. Berger. "The Feminist Self-Defense Movement: A Case Study." *Gender and Society* 1 (1987) 61–84.

Shaffer, Thomas L. *Moral Memoranda From John Howard Yoder: Conversations on Law, Ethics and the Church Between a Mennonite Theologian and a Hoosier Lawyer.* Eugene, OR: Wipf & Stock, 2002.

Smith, Michael B. *Toward the Outside: Concepts and Themes in Emmanuel Levinas.* Pittsburgh: Duquesne University Press, 2005.

Smith, Steven G. *The Argument to the Other: Reason Beyond Reason in the Thought of Karl Barth and Emmanuel Levinas.* Chico, CA: Scholars, 1983.

Smith. Columbia, NY: Columbia University Press, 1999.

Soskice, Janet Martin, and Diana Lipton. *Feminism & Theology.* Oxford: Oxford University Press, 2003.

Stassen, Glen H. *Just Peacemaking: Transforming Initiatives for Justice and Peace.* Louisville: Westminster John Knox, 1992.

Stout, Jeffrey. *Democracy and Tradition.* Princeton, NJ: Princeton University Press, 2004.

———. *Ethics After Babel: The Languages of Morals and Their Discontents.* Edition with New Postscript. Princeton, NJ: Princeton University Press, 2001.

Tilley, Terrence W. "Faith Based Initiator." *Commonweal* 131 (2004) 29–31.

Troeltsch, Ernst. *The Social Teaching of the Christian Churches.* 2 vols. Translated by Olive Wyon. New York: Harper & Row, 1960.

U.S. Catholic Bishops. "The Challenge of Peace: God's Promise and Our Response." *Catholic Social Thought*, editors. David J. O'Brien et al., 489–571. Maryknoll, NY: Orbis, 1992.

Virilio, Paul. *Speed and Politics: An Essay on Dromology.* Translated by Mark Polizzotti. Los Angeles: Semiotext(e), 2006.

Virilio, Paul, and Sylvere Lotringer. *Pure War: Twenty-Five Years Later.* Translated by Mark Polizzotti. Los Angeles: Semiotext(e), 2008.

Weaver, Alain Epp. "After Politics: John Howard Yoder, Body Politics, and the Witnessing Church." *The Review of Politics* 61 (1999) 637–73.

———. "On Exile: Yoder, Said, and a Theology of Land and Return." *Cross Currents* 52 (2003) 439–61.

Weaver, J. Denny. *The Nonviolent Atonement.* Grand Rapids: Eerdmans, 2001.

Wells, Samuel. *Transforming Fate into Destiny: The Theological Ethics of Stanley Hauerwas.* Eugene, OR: Cascade, 2004.

Wright, Nigel Goring. *Disavowing Constantine: Mission, Church and the Social Order in the Theologies of John Howard Yoder and Jürgen Moltmann.* Carlisle: Paternoster, 2000.

Wyschogrod, Edith. *Emmanuel Levinas: The Problem of Ethical Metaphysics.* NY: Fordham University Press, 2000.

———. "God and 'Being's Move' in the Philosophy of Emmanuel Levinas." *The Journal of Religion* 62 (1982) 145–55.

Yoder, John Howard. *Anabaptism and Reformation in Switzerland: An Historical and Theological Analysis of the Dialogues Between Anabaptists and Reformers.* Translated by David Carl Stassen and C. Arnold Snyder. Kitchener: Pandora, 2004.

———. "Anabaptist Vision and Mennonite Reality." In *Consultation On Anabaptist Mennonite Theology*, edited by A. J. Klassen, 1–46. Fresno, CA: The Council of Mennonite Seminaries, 1970.

———. "Armaments and Eschatology." *Studies in Christian Ethics* 1 (1998) 43–61.

———. *Body Politics: Five Practices of the Christian Community Before the Watching World*. Nashville: Discipleship Resources, 1994.
———. "The Burden and the Discipline of Evangelical Revisionism." In *Nonviolent America: History Through the Eyes of Peace*, edited by Louise Hawkey and James C. Juhnke, 21–37. Newton, KS: Mennonite, 1993.
———. "The Christian and Capital Punishment." In *Institute of Mennonite Studies*. 1 (1961) 1–23.
———. *The Christian Witness to the State*. Scottdale, PA: Herald, 2002.
———. "The Conditions of Countercultural Credibility." In *The Making of an Economic Vision*, edited by Oliver F. Williams and John W. Houck, 261–74. Lanham, MD: University Press of America, 1991.
———. *Discipleship as Political Responsibility*. Scottdale, PA: Herald, 2003.
———. "Ethics and Eschatology." *Ex Auditu* 6 (1990) 119–28.
———. *For The Nations: Essays Public & Evangelical*. Grand Rapids: Eerdmans, 1997.
———. *The Fullness of Christ: Paul's Vision of Universal Ministry*. Elgin, IL: Brethren, 1987.
———. *He Came Preaching Peace*. Scottdale, PA: Herald, 1985.
———. "How Many Ways are There to Think Morally About War?." *Journal of Law and Religion* 11 (1994–1995) 83–107.
———. *The Jewish-Christian Schism Revisited*. Edited by Michael G. Cartwright and Peter Ochs. Grand Rapids: Eerdmans, 2003.
———. *Karl Barth and the Problem of War: And Other Essays on Barth*. Edited by Mark Thiessen Nation. Eugene, OR: Cascade, 2003.
———. *The Legacy of Michael Sattler*. Scottdale, PA: Herald, 1973.
———. "Meaning After Babble: With Jeffrey Stout Beyond Relativism." *Journal Of Religious Ethics* 24 (1996) 125–39.
———. "Neither Guerrilla nor *Conquista*: The Presence of the Kingdom as Social Ethic." In *Peace, Politics, and the People of God*, edited by Paul Peachey, 95–116. Philadelphia: Fortress, 1986.
———. *Nevertheless: Varieties of Religious Pacifism*. Scottdale, PA: Herald, 1992.
———. "On Not Being Ashamed of the Gospel: Particularity, Pluralism, and Validation." *Faith and Philosophy* 9 (1992) 285–300.
———. "On Not Being in Charge." In *War and Its Discontents*, edited by J. Patout Burns, 74–90. Washington, DC: Georgetown University Press, 1996.
———. *The Original Revolution: Essays on Christian Pacifism*. Eugene, OR: Wipf & Stock, 1998.
———. *The Politics of Jesus*. 2nd ed. Grand Rapids: Eerdmans, 1994.
———. *Preface to Theology*. Grand Rapids: Brazos, 2002.
———. *The Priestly Kingdom: Social Ethics as Gospel*. Notre Dame, IN: University of Notre Dame Press, 1984.
———. *The Royal Priesthood: Essays Ecclesiastical and Ecumenical*. Edited by Michael G. Cartwright. Scottdale, PA: Herald, 1998.
———. "Surrender: A Moral Imperative." *The Review of Politics* 48 (1986) 576–95.
———. "Theological Revision and the Burden of Particular Identity." In *James M. Gustafson's Theocentric Ethics: Interpretations and Assessments*, edited by Harlan R. Beckley and Charles M. Sweezey, 63–94. Macon, GA: Mercer University Press, 1988.
———. "Three Ways to Respect Life." In *The Evangelical Roundtable: The Sanctity of Life*, edited by David A. Fraser, 92–100. Princeton, NJ: Princeton University Press, 1988.

Bibliography

———. "The Unique Role of the Historic Peace Churches." *Brethren Life and Thought* 50 (2005) 80–99.

———. *To Hear The Word*. Eugene, OR: Wipf & Stock, 2001.

———. "Walk and Word: The Alternatives to Methodologism." In *Theology Without Foundations: Religious Practice & the Future of Theological Truth*, edited by Stanley Hauerwas, Nancey Murphy, and Mark Nation, 77–90. Nashville: Abingdon, 1994.

———. "War as a Moral Problem in the Early Church: The Historian's Hermeneutical Assumptions." In *The Pacifist Impulse in Historical Perspective*, edited by Harvey L. Dyck, 90–110. Toronto: University of Toronto Press, 1996.

———. *What Would You Do?*. Scottdale, PA: Herald, 1992.

———. *When War is Unjust: Being Honest in Just War Thinking*. Eugene, OR: Wipf & Stock, 2001.

———. "Withdrawal and Diaspora: Two Faces of Liberation." In *Freedom and Discipleship: Liberation Theology in Anabaptist Perspective*, edited by Daniel S. Schipani, 76–84. Maryknoll, NY: Orbis, 1989.

Yoder, John Howard, Douglas Gwyn, George Hunsinger, and Eugene F. Roop. *A Declaration on Peace: In God's People the World's Renewal has Begun*. Scottdale, PA: Herald, 1991.

Yoder, John Howard, Glen H. Stassen, and D. M. Yeager. *Authentic Transformation: A New Vision of Christ and Culture*. Nashville: Abingdon, 1996.

Zimmerman, Earl. *Practicing the Politics of Jesus: The Origin and Significance of John Howard Yoder's Social Ethics*. Telford, PA: Cascadia, 2007.

Index

Andolsen, Barbara, 132
Aquinas, Thomas, 46, 65
Aristotle, 48, 60, 65
Augustine, 46
Batnitzky, Leora, 133
De Beauvoir, Simone, 134
Biblical Realism, 12, 15
Blum, Peter, 87
Bohn, Carole R., 132
Boyarin, Daniel, 124–25
Brown, Joanne Carlson, 132
Burggraeve, Roger, 130–31
Cahill, Lisa Sowle, 37n12
Carter, Craig, 6, 8, 10, 32–34, 37–38, 57, 58–64, 73–74, 82–83, 85
Cartwright, Michael, 122
Chanter, Tina, 134–35
Coles, Romand, 70–73
Constantinian, 44–46, 58, 75, 122–23
Cross, Crucifixion, 23–24, 28–29, 54
Deats, Paul, 36
Derrida, Jacques, 74, 76, 129
Dibelius, Martin, 21
Discipleship, 9–10, 20–21, 23–25, 29–30, 108
Donahue, John, 31–33
Epictetus, 17
Foucault, Michel, 74, 76, 80, 82
Gustafson, James, 34, 37–43, 47, 51–54, 57, 65, 68–70, 73, 80, 83, 113, 119

Hauerwas, Stanley, 6, 8, 10, 54, 64–74, 82–85, 125
Haustafeln, Household Codes, Precepts, 21–23, 26, 28, 47–48, 54, 113–15
Heidegger, Martin, 95
Huebner, Chris K., 6, 8, 57–58, 73–82, 84–85, 87–93
Husserl, Edmund, 91-92, 95
Irigaray, Luce, 134–35
Judaism, 7–8, 46, 108–9, 120–28
Katz, Claire, 135–36
Kavka, Martin, 90–93
Kenosis, 7–8, 88, 108–11, 119, 121
Kepnes, Steven, 127
Klassen, William, 1
Kroeker, Travis, 63
Levinas, Emmanuel, 4–5, 7–8
Lindbeck, George, 58, 60, 63
Littell, Franklin H., 35n8
MacIntyre, Alasdair, 65–67, 69–71, 84
Methodologism, 16–19, 112–13, 117–18
Middle Axioms, 3, 126
Murphy, Nancey, 75
Nation, Mark, 1–2, 4, 32–34, 117
Ochs, Peter, 122, 124
Plato, 60
Reimer, A. James, 34, 43–47, 51, 57–62, 64, 80, 83, 119

Index

Revolutionary Subordination, 5, 8–10, 20–23, 26–30, 47–48, 54, 80–82, 113–15, 117–18, 137
Reuther, Rosemary, 132
Robinson, John, 62–63
Rose, Gillian, 87–93
Schussler Fiorenza, Elizabeth, 34, 47–49, 51, 54, 57, 80–81, 119

Schwarzschild, Steven, 122
Schweitzer, Albert, 11–12
Sectarian, and Sect, 5–6, 33–37, 49, 55, 68–69, 87–88
Stout, Jeffrey, 19–20
Troeltsch, Ernst, 35, 55
Virilio, Paul, 77–79, 82
Wyschogrod, Edith, 127

www.ingramcontent.com/pod-product-compliance
Lightning Source LLC
Chambersburg PA
CBHW070907160426
43193CB00011B/1389